Anonymous

Organization, Articles of Association and Consolidation

And acts of Congress and of the Legislature of the State of California

relative thereto

Anonymous

Organization, Articles of Association and Consolidation
And acts of Congress and of the Legislature of the State of California relative thereto

ISBN/EAN: 9783337233648

Printed in Europe, USA, Canada, Australia, Japan

Cover: Foto ©Suzi / pixelio.de

More available books at **www.hansebooks.com**

Southern Pacific Railroad

COMPANY.

•—•—•

ORGANIZATION.

—•—•—•—

Articles of Association and Consolidation,

AND

Acts of Congress and of the Legislature of the State of California relative thereto.

[COMPILED FROM AUTHENTIC SOURCES.]

New York. 1875.

— ◆ —

NEW YORK:
EVENING POST STEAM PRESSES, 41 NASSAU STREET, CORNER LIBERTY.

1875.

TABLE OF CONTENTS.

———◆◆◆———

iv

TABLE OF CONTENTS OF SUPPLEMENT.

————▶◆◀————

Southern Pacific Railroad Company.

ORGANIZATION.

{ L. B. H. 5 cts. Int. Rev. }
{ Stamp. April 10, '71. }

I.

The San Francisco and San José Railroad Company.

*Certified Copy Articles of Association and Acceptance of
Provisions of Act of May 20th, 1861, Certified
List of Officers and Copy of Resolution
to Consolidate with Other Roads.*

STATE OF CALIFORNIA, }
    Department of State. }

I, H. L. Nichols, Secretary of State of the State of California,
do hereby certify that the annexed is a true, full and correct
copy of Articles of Association of the San Francisco and San
José Railroad Company, with endorsements thereon, now on
file in my office.

    Witness my hand, and the great seal of State, at
    office in Sacramento, California, the tenth day
{ Seal }
{ of State. }   of April, A. D. 1871.

              H. L. NICHOLS,
                      Secretary of State.

By LEW. B. HARRIS,
        Deputy.

COPY OF ARTICLES OF ASSOCIATION OF THE SAN FRANCISCO & SAN JOSE RAILROAD COMPANY.

Know all men by these Presents : That we, the undersigned, being subscribers to the stock of a contemplated railroad from the city of San Francisco, in the county of San Francisco and State of California, through said county and the counties of San Mateo and Santa Clara to the city of San José, in said State ; which stock, subscribed by us, amounts to at least one thousand dollars for every mile of the railroad intended to be built, and, which stock has been by us subscribed in good faith, and more than ten per cent. in cash paid thereon to Charles McLaughlin, who has been by us appointed temporary Treasurer; and being desirous of forming a corporation, do hereby, at a regular meeting of said stockholders, held pursuant to due notice thereof in writing, given by said Treasurer, adopt the following

ARTICLES OF ASSOCIATION.

Article 1.—We, the undersigned, whose names are hereto subscribed, do hereby organize, form and become a corporation and body corporate under and in pursuance of an Act of the Legislature of the State of California, entitled "An Act to provide for the Incorporation of Railroad Companies," passed April 22, A. D. 1853, and of the several acts supplementary to and amendatory thereof, for the purpose of constructing, owning and maintaining a railroad from the city of San Francisco, in the county of San Francisco, through said county and the counties of San Mateo and Santa Clara to the city of San José, all in the said State of California, to be known by the name of "The San Francisco and San Jose Railroad Company," to continue in existence for the term of fifty years from the date hereof.

Article 2.—The capital stock of said corporation shall be, and is, hereby fixed at two millions of dollars, being the actual cost of constructing said railroad, the cost of right-of-way, motive-power, and every other appurtenance for the completion and running of said road, as estimated by competent engineers, and shall consist of and be divided into twenty thousand shares of one hundred dollars each.

Article 3.—The number of Directors to manage the concerns of said corporation shall be seven, and the names of the persons chosen to act as such Directors, and to hold their offices until others are duly elected, are James A. McDougall, Charles McLaughlin, Timothy Dame, Charles L. Weller, Henry M. Newhall, Timothy G. Phelps and George H. Bodfish, all of whom are subscribers to these Articles of Association.

Article 4.—The length of said proposed railroad, as nearly as the same can now be ascertained, will be forty-eight miles.

Article 5.—The five persons who have been selected and are hereby designated as Commissioners to open books of subscription for the stock of said corporation are D. S. Cook, C. E. Allen, Charles McLaughlin, William J. Lewis and Hugh O'Donnell, all of whom are subscribers to these Articles of Association.

In witness whereof, we have hereunto severally subscribed our names and places of residence this twenty-first day of July, in the year one thousand eight hundred and sixty.

NAMES.	RESIDENCE.	NUMBER OF SHARES.
J. A. McDougall	San Francisco	Fifty.
Chas. McLaughlin	San Francisco	One hundred.
A. H. Houston	San Francisco	Fifteen.
William J. Lewis	San Francisco	Twenty.
John Middleton	San Francisco	Ten.
T. G. Phelps	San Mateo	Five.
C. L. Weller	San Francisco	Twenty.
Robt. E. Hunter	Hunter's Point	Ten.
H. M. Newhall	San Francisco	Twenty.
B. F. Mann	San José	One hundred.
John H. Atchinson	Yuba County	One hundred.
Timothy Dame	San Francisco	Fifty.
C. E. Allen	San José	Ten.
W. B. Farwell	San Francisco	Five.
Jno. V. Wattson	San Francisco	Ten.
E. A. Rockwell	San Francisco	Ten.
Fred'k A. Benjamin	San Francisco	Five.
J. F. Bowman	San Francisco	Five.
H. O. Donnell	San Francisco	Twenty-five.
Rich. Roman	San Francisco	Five.
D. S. Cook	San Mateo	Five.
Geo. D. Nagle	San Francisco	10) Ten.
Jasper Babcock	San Francisco	5) Five.
H. W. Seale	May Field	50) Fifty.
Sam'l H. Dwinelle	San Francisco	10) Ten.
Geo. H. Bodfish	San José	Five.
Myles D. Sweeny	San Francisco	Five.
Wm. Schmolz	San Francisco	Five.

THE STATE OF CALIFORNIA, } ss. :
City and County of San Francisco, }

On this twenty-fourth day of July, A. D. 1860, personally appeared before me, the undersigned, a notary public in and for said city and county, James A. McDougall, Charles Mc-Laughlin and Timothy Dame, three of the Directors of "The San Francisco & San Jose Railroad Company," duly elected by the stockholders of said Company, and who, being severally duly sworn, on their oaths do say, that over one thousand dol-lars for each mile of the railroad proposed and mentioned in the foregoing Articles of Association, has actually and in good faith been subscribed to the stock of said Company by the persons whose names appear subscribed to the said Articles of Association; and that more than ten per cent. on said amount, namely, five thousand seven hundred and fifty dollars, has actually been paid in cash to Charles McLaughlin, the Treas-urer appointed by the Directors named in the foregoing Arti-cles, and that the subscribers to the said Articles of Association are all known to them and each of them, to be subscribers thereto, and to be the persons so represented.

(Signed)   J. A. McDOUGALL.
CHAS. McLAUGHLIN.
TIMOTHY DAME.

Subscribed and sworn to before me, the day and year last above written.

[L. S.]   In testimony whereof, I have hereunto subscribed my name and affixed my notarial seal, this twenty-fourth day of July, A. D. 1860.

(Signed)   E. P. PECKHAM,
Notary Public.

(Endorsed.)

San Francisco and San José Railroad Company.
Filed August 18th, 1860.—Fees $10, paid.
Recorded in Book B, folio 703.

Know all men by these presents, that "The San Francisco and San José Railroad Company," a corporation now in legal existence, which was duly organized by Articles of Association, dated July 21st, A. D. 1860, under and in pursuance of "An Act of the Legislature of the State of California, entitled an Act to provide for the incorporation of railroad companies," passed April 22d, A. D. 1853, and of the several acts supplementary to and amendatory thereof, for the purpose of constructing, owning and maintaining a railroad from the city of San Francisco, in the county of San Francisco, through said county and the counties of San Mateo and Santa Clara to the city of San José, all in the said State of California : does hereby accept of all the provisions, powers, rights, benefits, obligations and restrictions of an Act of the Legislature of said State of California, entitled " An Act to provide for the Incorporation of Railroad Companies, and the management of the affairs thereof, and other matters relating thereto," approved May 20th, A. D. 1861, and does hereby fully surrender the Act or Acts, under which the said Company was organized ; provided, however, that this acceptance of said Act of May 20th, A. D. 1861, shall in nowise affect any rights, powers, franchises or privileges obtained or now enjoyed by said Company under any law of said State in force before the filing of this acceptance in the office of the Secretary of State, as provided in section 56 of said Act, approved May 20th, A. D. 1861.

In witness whereof, the Directors of said Company have hereunto signed their names and affixed the seal of said Company hereto, and the same is also attested by the President and Secretary thereof, at the office of said Company, in the city of San Francisco and State of California, this first day of July, A. D. 1861.

(Signed)   C. B. POLHEMUS,
PETER DONAHUE,
H. M. NEWHALL,
[SEAL.]   C. L. WELLER,
TIMOTHY DAME,
T. G. PHELPS,
GEO. H. BODFISH,

Directors of " The San Francisco and San José Railroad Company."

(Attest)   T. G. PHELPS,
President.

(Signed)   TIMOTHY DAME,
Secretary.

(Endorsed.)

San Francisco and San José R. R. Company, Acceptance of provisions of Act of May 20, 1861.

Filed July 8, 1861 ; filing, $5, paid.

THE SAN FRANCISCO AND SAN JOSE RAIL-ROAD COMPANY.

CERTIFIED LIST OF OFFICERS.

I, J. L. Willcutt, Secretary of the Southern Pacific Railroad Company, do hereby certify that at an annual meeting of the stockholders of " The San Francisco and San José Railroad Company," held in the city of San Francisco, on the 8th day of August, A. D. 1870, the following named persons were duly and legally elected Directors of said Company, to wit :

H. M. NEWHALL,	PETER DONAHUE,
CHARLES MAYNE,	W. C. RALSTON, .
JAMES O'NEILL,	MYLES D. SWEENY,
GILBERT PALACHE,	

and that at a meeting of said Directors regularly called and held on the day above mentioned, the following officers of said Company were duly and legally elected to serve during the ensuing year, to wit :

H. M. NEWHALL.........................President.
PETER DONAHUE.....................Vice President.
W. C. RALSTON........................Treasurer.
J. L. WILLCUTT........................Secretary.

The same appearing of record on the minutes of proceedings of the stockholders and Board of Directors of said Company.

[SEAL.]   In witness whereof, I have hereunto set my hand and affixed the corporate seal of the Company, this thirteenth day of April, A. D. 1871.

J. L. WILLCUTT,
Secy. So. Pacific R. R. Co.

RESOLUTION OF

THE SAN FRANCISCO AND SAN JOSE RAILROAD COMPANY TO
CONSOLIDATE WITH OTHER ROADS.

A meeting of the Board of Directors of The San Francisco and San José Railroad Company, regularly called, was held at the office of the Company, on the 11th day of October, A. D. 1870, all of the Directors being present, to wit:

H. M. NEWHALL,   PETER DONAHUE,
CHAS. MAYNE,   W. C. RALSTON,
MYLES D. SWEENY,   GILBERT PALACHE,
              and JAS. O'NEILL.

Mr. Newhall, presiding as President of the Board.

The President announced the special object of the meeting, whereupon Mr. Donahue offered the following resolution, to wit:

Resolved, That this corporation do consolidate with the Santa Clara and Pajaro Valley Railroad Company, the California Southern Railroad Company and the Southern Pacific Railroad Company, upon the terms and conditions set forth in the Articles of Association, Amalgamation and Consolidation, now herewith presented, which are hereby approved, and the President and Secretary of this Company are hereby authorized and required to subscribe the name of this corporation to said articles and affix its corporate seal thereto, and deliver said articles as the act and deed of this corporation.

Which resolution was adopted by the unanimous vote and concurrence of the full Board of Directors, the articles referred to in this resolution being as follows, to wit:

(ARTICLES OF ASSOCIATION, AMALGAMATION AND CONSOLIDATION, Dated October 11th, 1870, as per accompanying certified copy.)

I, J. L. Willcutt, Secretary of the Southern Pacific Railroad Company, hereby certify the foregoing to be a true and correct copy from the minutes of the proceedings of the Board of Directors of the San Francisco and San José Railroad Company.

                In witness whereof, I have hereunto set my hand
[SEAL.]   and affixed the corporate seal of the company,
                this thirteenth day of April A. D. 1871.

                          J. L. WILLCUTT,
                        Secy. So. Pacific R. R. Co.

II.

SOUTHERN PACIFIC RAILROAD COMPANY.

(Old Organization.)

CERTIFIED COPY ARTICLES OF ASSOCIATION—CERTIFIED LIST OF OFFICERS AND COPY RESOLUTION TO CONSOLIDATE WITH OTHER COMPANIES.

———

STATE OF CALIFORNIA, }
Department of State. }

{ L. D. H.
Five cents Int.
Rev. Stamp.
April 10, 1871. } I, H. L. Nichols, Secretary of State of the State of California, do hereby certify that the annexed is a true, full and correct copy of Articles of Association of the Southern Pacific Railroad Company, with endorsements now on file in my office.

{ Seal of
State. } Witness my hand and the great seal of State, at office in Sacramento, California, the tenth day of April, A. D. 1871.

H. L. NICHOLS,
Secretary of State.
by LEW. B. HARRIS,
Deputy.

———

SOUTHERN PACIFIC RAILROAD COMPANY.

ARTICLES OF ASSOCIATION.

Know all men by these presents, That we, the undersigned, being subscribers to the stock of a contemplated railroad from some point on the bay of San Francisco, in the State of California, through the counties of Santa Clara, Monterey, San Luis Obispo, Tulare, Los Angeles and San Diego, to the town of San Diego, in said State; thence eastward through the said

county of San Diego to the eastern line of the State of California, there to connect with a contemplated railroad from said
eastern line of the State of California to the Mississippi river;
which stock subscribed by us amounts to, at least, one thousand dollars for each and every mile of said proposed railroad,
and of which ten per cent. in cash has been actually and in
good faith paid thereon to B. W. Hathaway, one of our number, who has been by us appointed temporary Treasurer, and
being desirous of forming a corporation, do hereby, at
a regular meeting of said stockholders, held pursuant to due
notice thereof, in writing, given by said Treasurer, adopt the
following

ARTICLES OF ASSOCIATION.

ARTICLE 1. We, the undersigned, whose names are hereto subscribed, do hereby organize, form and become a corporation
and body politic, under and in pursuance of an Act of the
Legislature of the State of California, entitled "An Act to
provide for the Incorporation of Railroad Companies, and the
management of the affairs thereof, and other matters relating
thereto," approved May 20, A. D. 1861, and the several Acts
supplementary to and amendatory thereof, for the purpose of
constructing, owning and maintaining a railroad from some point
on the bay of San Francisco, in the State of California, and to
pass through the counties of Santa Clara, Monterey, San Luis
Obispo, Tularo, Los Angeles and San Diego, to the town of San
Diego, in said State; thence eastward through the said county of
San Diego to the eastern line of the State of California, there to
connect with a contemplated railroad from said eastern line of
the State of California to the Mississippi river.

ARTICLE 2. The name of the corporation hereby formed and
organized shall be "Southern Pacific Railroad Company,"
and the same shall continue in existence for the term of fifty
years from the date hereof.

ARTICLE 3. The length of said proposed railroad, as near as
may be, is seven hundred and twenty miles.

ARTICLE 4. The capital stock of said corporation shall be, and
is, hereby fixed at thirty millions dollars, being the actual con-

templated cost of constructing said railroad, together with the cost of the right-of-way, motive-power and every other appurtenance and thing necessary for the completion and running of said road, as near as can be estimated by competent engineers, and shall consist of, and be divided into, three hundred thousand shares of one hundred dollars each.

ARTICLE 5. The number of Directors to manage the affairs of said corporation shall be seven, and the names of the persons chosen to act as such Directors, and to hold their offices until others are duly elected, are T. G. Phelps, Chas. N. Fox, Benjamin Flint, C. J. Hutchinson, B. G. Lathrop, J. B. Cox and B. W. Hathaway, all of whom are subscribers to these Articles of Association.

In testimony whereof, we have hereunto severally subscribed our names, places of residence and the number of said shares of stock held by each, this twenty-ninth day of November, 1865.

NAMES.	RESIDENCE.	NO. OF SHARES.
T. G. Phelps.............	San Francisco......	(720) Seven hundred & twenty.
Chas. N. Fox.............	San Mateo.........	(720) Seven hundred & twenty.
B. G. Lathrop...........	San Mateo.........	(720) Seven hundrel & twenty.
Benjamin Flint..........	San Juan.........	(720) Seven hundred & twenty.
C. J. Hutchinson........	San Francisco.....	(720) Seven hundred & twenty.
W. S. Rosecrans, by J. B.		
Cox, his att'y. in fact....	Cincinnati, O.......	(720) Seven hundred & twenty.
J. B. Cox...............	San Francisco......	(720) Seven hundred & twenty.
B. W. Hathaway.........	San Francisco	(720) Seven hundred & twenty.
John F. Sears...........	San Francisco......	(720) Seven hundred & twenty.
Wm. T. Coleman.........	San Francisco......	(720) Seven hundred & twenty.
J. W. Stephenson........	San Francisco......	(720) Seven hundred & twenty.

STATE OF CALIFORNIA, }
City and County of San Francisco, } ss.:

T. G. Phelps, Benjamin Flint and B. W. Hathaway being duly sworn, do depose and say: That they are, and each of them is, a director of the "Southern Pacific Railroad Company," that at least one thousand dollars for each and every mile of the railroad, proposed and mentioned in the foregoing Articles of Association, to wit : Seven hundred and twenty thousand dollars, has actually and in good faith been subscribed to the capital stock of said Company by the persons whose names appear subscribed to said Articles of Association, and that ten per cent. on said amount so subscribed has actually and in good faith been paid to B. W. Hathaway, the Treasurer, named and appointed by said subscribers from among their number, and that the said subscribers are known to these deponents, and to each of them, to be subscribers to said Articles of Association, and to be the persons so represented.

T. G. PHELPS.
BENJAMIN FLINT.
B. W. HATHAWAY.

Subscribed and sworn to before me, ⎫
   this 29th day of November, 1865, ⎭

GEO. C. WALLER,

[SEAL.]   Not. Pub.

⎧ 5 cent In. Rev. stamp, ⎫
⎨   G. C. W.   ⎬
⎩ Nov. 29, 1865. ⎭

(Endorsed.)

Southern Pacific Railway Company. Articles of Association. Filed in office of Secretary of State, Dec. 2d, 1865. Fees, $5.00. Pd.

SOUTHERN PACIFIC RAILROAD COMPANY.

(Old Organization.)

CERTIFIED LIST OF OFFICERS.

I, J. L. Willcutt, Secretary of the Southern Pacific Railroad Company, hereby certify that at an annual meeting of the stockholders of said Company, held in the city of San José, county of Santa Clara, on the 12th day of January, A.D. 1870, the following named persons were duly and legally elected Directors of said Company, to wit:

LLOYD TEVIS,	EDGAR MILLS,
LEWIS CUNNINGHAM,	WM. E. BARRON,
D. O. MILLS,	THOMAS BELL,

and HENRY E. ROBINSON.

And that at a meeting of said Directors, regularly called and held in the city of San Francisco, on the 8th day of February. A. D. 1870, the following officers of said Company were duly and legally elected, to wit:

LLOYD TEVIS, President.	D. O. MILLS, Vice-President.
EDGAR MILLS, Treasurer.	B. B. MINOR, Secretary.

And further, that at a meeting of the Board of Directors of said Company, regularly called, and held on the 4th day of May, A. D. 1870, the written resignation of Henry E. Robinson and Lewis Cunningham, Directors of the Company, were presented and accepted, and that James B. Haggin and Wm. B. Carr were duly and legally elected Directors to fill the unexpired term of said Henry E. Robinson and Lewis Cunningham, the same appearing of record on the minutes of the proceedings of the stockholders and Board of Directors of said Company.

[SEAL.] In witness whereof, I have hereunto set my hand and affixed the corporate seal of the Company, this thirteenth day of April, A. D. 1871.

J. L. WILLCUTT,
Sec'y So. Pacific R. R. Co.

SOUTHERN PACIFIC RAILROAD COMPANY.

RESOLUTION TO CONSOLIDATE WITH OTHER COMPANIES.

I, J. L. Willcutt, Secretary of the Southern Pacific Railroad Company, hereby certify that a meeting of the Board of Directors of said Company, regularly called, was held in the city of San Francisco, on the 11th day of October, A. D. 1870, and that, among other proceedings, the following resolution was unanimously adopted, to wit:

" *Resolved and Ordered,* That this Company do consolidate with "The San Francisco and San José Railroad Company, the Santa Clara and Pajaro Valley Railroad Company and the California Southern Railroad Company, upon the terms and conditions set forth in the Articles of Association, Amalgamation and Consolidation, now herewith presented, and which are hereby approved, and the President and Secretary of this Company be, and they are, hereby authorized and required to affix the corporate seal of this Company thereto, and sign and attest the same as the act and deed of this Company."

(The articles referred to are the "Articles of Association, Amalgamation and Consolidation," as per certified copy herewith.)

[SEAL.]   In witness whereof, I have hereunto set my name and affixed the corporate seal of the Company, this thirteenth day of April, A. D. 1871.

J. L. WILLCUTT,
Sec'y So. Pacific R. R. Co.

III.

SANTA CLARA AND PAJARO VALLEY RAILROAD COMPANY.

CERTIFIED COPY ARTICLES OF ASSOCIATION—CERTIFIED LIST OF OFFICERS AND COPY RESOLUTION TO CONSOLIDATE WITH OTHER COMPANIES.

STATE OF CALIFORNIA, }
Department of State. }

I, H. L. Nichols, Secretary of State of the State of California, do hereby certify that the annexed is a true, full and correct copy of Articles of Association of the Santa Clara and

3

Pajaro Valley Railroad Company, with endorsements thereon, now on file in my office.

{Seal of State.}

Witness my hand and the great seal of State, at office in Sacramento, California, the tenth day of April, A. D. 1871.

H. L. Nichols,
Secretary of State.

{5c. Int. Rev. Stamp. L. B. H. April 10, 1871.}

By Lew. B. Harris,
Deputy.

ARTICLES OF ASSOCIATION

OF THE

SANTA CLARA AND PAJARO VALLEY RAILROAD CO.

Know all men by these presents, That we, the undersigned, being the subscribers to the stock of a contemplated railroad from a point at or near the city of San Jose, in the county of Santa Clara and State of California, to a point at or near the town of New Gilroy, in the same county, said railroad being wholly within said county of Santa Clara, which stock subscribed by us amounts to at least one thousand dollars for each and every mile of the said proposed railroad, and ten per cent. in cash has been actually and in good faith paid thereon to Jos. L. Willcutt, one of our number, who has been by us appointed Treasurer, and being desirous of forming a corporation, do hereby, at a regular meeting of said stockholders, held pursuant to due notice thereof, in writing, given by said Treasurer, adopt the following

ARTICLES OF ASSOCIATION :

ARTICLE 1. We, the undersigned, whose names are hereto subscribed, do hereby organize, form and become a corporation and body politic and corporate, under and in pursuance of an Act of the Legislature of the State of California, entitled " An Act to provide for the Incorporation of Railroad Companies, and the management of the affairs thereof, and other matters relating thereto," approved May 20th, A. D. 1861; and of the several acts supplementary to and amendatory thereof, for the purpose of constructing, owning and maintaining a railroad from a point at or near the city of San José, in the county of Santa Clara, connecting at such point with the San Francisco and San José Railroad, and to pass to a point at or near the town of New Gilroy, in the same county, said Railroad being wholly within the limits of said county of Santa Clara, in the State of California.

ARTICLE 2. The name of the corporation hereby formed and organized shall be the " Santa Clara and Pajaro Valley Railroad Company," and the same shall continue in existence for the term of fifty years from the date hereof.

ARTICLE 3. The length of said proposed railroad (as near as may be), is thirty (30) miles.

ARTICLE 4. The capital stock of said corporation shall be, and is, hereby fixed at one million dollars, being the actual contemplated cost of constructing said railroad, together with the cost of the right-of-way, motive power, and every other appurtenance and thing for the completion and running of said road, as nearly as can be estimated by competent engineers, and shall consist of and be divided into ten thousand shares of one hundred dollars each.

ARTICLE 5. The number of Directors to manage the affairs of said corporation or Company shall be five, and the names of the persons chosen to act as such Directors, and hold their offices until others are duly elected, are Charles Mayne, Peter Donahue, Richard P. Hammond, Henry M. Newhall and Myles D. Sweeny, all of whom are subscribers to these Articles of Association.

> In witness whereof, we have hereunto severally subscribed our names, places of residence and the number of said shares of stock held by each, this 31st day of December, A. D. one thousand eight hundred and sixty-seven (1867).

NAMES.	RESIDENCE.	NO. OF SHARES.
H. M. Newhall	San Francisco	3,166
Peter Donahue	do.	3,167
Chas. Mayne	do.	3,167
H. Barroilhet	do.	100
Myles D. Sweeny	do.	100
J. O. Eldridge	do.	100
Edward Martin	do.	50
Jas. O'Niell	do.	50
Richard P. Hammond	do.	50
Jos. L. Willcutt	do.	50

STATE OF CALIFORNIA, ⎫
City and County of San Francisco, ⎬ ss. :

On this thirty-first day of December, A. D. 1867, personally appeared before me, a notary public in and for said city and county, Myles D. Sweeny, Richard P. Hammond and H. M. Newhall, three of the Directors of the Santa Clara and Pajaro Valley Railroad Company named in the Articles of Association hereto attached, and who being by me severally duly sworn, on their oaths do say, that over one thousand dollars for each and every mile of the railroad proposed and mentioned in the said articles of association, to wit, The sum of one million dollars, has actually and in good faith been subscribed to the stock of the Company by the persons whose names appear subscribed to the said Articles of Association, and that ten per cent. on said amount so subscribed, namely, the sum of one hundred thousand dollars, has actually and in good faith been paid to Joseph L. Willcutt, the Treasurer named and appointed by said subscribers from among their number, and that the said subscribers are all known to said three Directors, and to each of them, to be subscribers to said Articles of Association, and to be the persons so represented.

H. M. NEWHALL.

MYLES D. SWEENY.

, RICHARD P. HAMMOND.

Subscribed and sworn to before me, the day and year last above written. In testimony whereof, I have hereunto subscribed my name and affixed my notarial seal this thirty-first day of December, A. D. 1867.

[SEAL.]

SAMUEL HERMANN,
Notary Public.

(Endorsed)—Articles of Association of the Santa Clara and Pajaro Valley Railroad Co.—Filed in office of the Secretary of State, January 2d, 1868.

: 5 cent Int. Rev. :
: stamp. H. L. N. :
: January 2, '68. :

H. L. NICHOLS,
Sec. of State.

By LEW. B. HARRIS,
Deputy.

$5.00 fees, paid.

SANTA CLARA AND PAJARO VALLEY RAILROAD COMPANY.

CERTIFIED LIST OF OFFICERS.

I, J. L. Willcutt, Secretary of the Southern Pacific Railroad Company, hereby certify that at an annual meeting of the stockholders of the Santa Clara and Pajaro Valley Railroad Company, held in the town of Gilroy, Santa Clara county, on the 16th day of April, A. D. 1870, the following named persons were duly and legally elected Directors of said Company, to wit:

PETER DONAHUE,   H. M. NEWHALL,
CHARLES MAYNE,   MYLES D. SWEENY,
            and RICHARD P. HAMMOND,

and that at a meeting of said Directors held immediately after the adjournment of said stockholders' meeting, the following persons were duly and legally elected officers of the Company, to serve for the ensuing year:

PETER DONAHUE was elected President,
CHARLES MAYNE was elected Vice-President,
MYLES D. SWEENY was elected Treasurer,
J. L. WILLCUTT was elected Secretary,

as appears of record on the minutes of proceedings of the stockholders and Board of Directors of said Company.

In witness whereof, I have hereunto set my hand
[SEAL.]   and affixed the corporate seal of the Company,
this thirteenth (13th) day of April, A. D. 1871.

J. L. WILLCUTT,
Secy. So. Pacific R.R. Co.

SANTA CLARA AND PAJARO VALLEY RAILROAD COMPANY.

RESOLUTION TO CONSOLIDATE WITH OTHER COMPANIES.

A meeting of the Board of Directors of the Santa Clara and Pajaro Valley Railroad Company, regularly called, was held at the Company's office on the 11th day of October, A. D. 1870, pursuant to the call of the President, the following Directors being present, to wit:

PETER DONAHUE,   H. M. NEWHALL,
CHARLES MAYNE,   MYLES D. SWEENY,
           and RICHARD P. HAMMOND.

Peter Donahue presiding as President of the Board.

The President announced the object of the meeting, whereupon Mr. Mayne offered the following resolution, to wit:

Resolved, That this corporation do consolidate with The San Francisco and San José Railroad Company, the California Southern Railroad Company and the Southern Pacific Railroad Company, upon the terms and conditions set forth in the Articles of Association, Amalgamation and Consolidation now herewith presented, which are hereby approved, and the President and Secretary of this Company are hereby authorized and required to subscribe the name of this corporation to said articles, and affix its corporate seal thereto, and deliver said articles as the act and deed of this corporation.

Which resolution was adopted by the unanimous vote and concurrence of the full Board of Directors.

The articles referred to in the resolution being as follows:

(Articles of Association, Amalgamation and Consolidation, as per accompanying certified copy.)

I, J. L. Willcutt, Secretary of the Southern Pacific Railroad Company, hereby certify the foregoing to be a true and correct copy of a resolution from the minutes of proceedings of the Board of Directors of the Santa Clara and Pajaro Valley Railroad Company.

              In witness whereof, I have hereunto set my hand
    [SEAL.]   and affixed the corporate seal of the Company,
              this thirteenth day of April, A. D. 1871.
                          J. L. WILLCUTT,
                          Secy. So. Pacific R.R. Co.

IV.

CALIFORNIA SOUTHERN RAILROAD COMPANY.

CERTIFIED COPY, ARTICLES OF ASSOCIATION—CERTIFIED LIST OF OFFICERS AND COPY RESOLUTION TO CONSOLIDATE WITH OTHER COMPANIES.

STATE OF CALIFORNIA, }
Department of State, }

I, H. L. Nichols, Secretary of State of the State of California, do hereby certify that the annexed is a true, full and correct copy of Articles of Association of the California Southern Railroad Company, with endorsements now on file in my office.

{ L. B. H. }
{ Five cent Int. }
{ Rev. Stamp. }
{ April 10, '71. }

Witness my hand and the great seal of State, at office in Sacramento, California, the tenth day of April, A. D. 1871.

{ Seal of }
{ State. }

H. L. NICHOLS,
Secretary of State.
By LEW. B. HARRIS,
Deputy.

ARTICLES OF ASSOCIATION

OF THE

CALIFORNIA SOUTHERN RAILROAD COMPANY.

Know all men by these presents, That we, the undersigned, being the subscribers to the stock of a contemplated railroad from a point at or near the town of Gilroy, in the county of Santa Clara, and State of California, to a point at or near the town of Salinas City, in the county of Monterey and said State of California, which stock subscribed by us amounts to at least one thousand dollars for each and every mile of the said proposed railroad; and ten per cent. in cash having been actually and in good faith paid thereon to Joseph L. Willcutt, one of our number, who has been by us appointed Treasurer, and being desirous of forming a corporation, do hereby, at a regular meeting of said stockholders, held pursuant to due notice thereof, in writing, given by said Treasurer, adopt the following:

ARTICLES OF ASSOCIATION.

ARTICLE I. We, the undersigned, whose names are hereto subscribed, do hereby organize, form and become a corporation and body politic and corporate, under and in pursuance of an Act of the Legislature of the State of California, entitled "An Act to provide for the Incorporation of Railroad Companies and the management of the affairs thereof, and other matters relating thereto," approved May 20th, A. D. 1861, and of the several Acts supplementary to and amendatory thereof, for the purpose of constructing, owning, and maintaining a railroad from a point at or near the town of Gilroy, in the county of Santa Clara, and to pass through the counties of Santa Clara, Santa Cruz and Monterey, to a point at or near the town of Salinas City, in said county of Monterey.

ARTICLE 2. The name of the corporation hereby formed and organized shall be the "California Southern Railroad Company," and the same shall continue in existence for the term of fifty years from the date hereof.

ARTICLE 3. The length of said proposed railroad (as near as may be) is forty-five miles.

ARTICLE 4. The capital stock of said corporation shall be, and is, hereby fixed at one million five hundred thousand dollars, being the actual contemplated cost of constructing said railroad, together with the cost of right-of-way, motive power, and every other appurtenance and thing for the completion and running of said road, as nearly as can be estimated by competent engineers, and shall consist of and be divided into fifteen thousand shares of one hundred dollars each.

ARTICLE 5. The number of Directors to manage the affairs of said corporation or company shall be five, and the names of the persons chosen to act as such Directors, and hold their offices until others are duly elected, are, Charles Mayne, Peter Donahue, Richard P. Hammond, Henry M. Newhall and Myles D. Sweeny, all of whom are subscribers to these Articles of Association.

In testimony whereof, we have hereunto severally subscribed our names, places of residence and the number of said shares of stock held by each, this   day of January, A. D. one thousand eight hundred and seventy.

NAMES.	RESIDENCE.	NO. OF SHARES.
Charles Mayne..............	San Francisco..............	4,767
Peter Donahue..............	do.	4,767
H. M. Newhall..............	do.	4,766
Richard P. Hammond........	do.	100
Edward Martin..............	do.	100
Myles D. Sweeny.............	San Francisco..............	100
J. O. Eldridge..............	San Francisco..............	100
H. Barroilhet	do.	100
G. Palache..................	do.	100
J. L. Willcutt..............	do.	100

STATE OF CALIFORNIA, } ss. :
City and County of San Francisco, }

On this 21st day of Jan., A. D. 1870, personally appeared before Samuel Hermann, a notary public in and for said city and county, Peter Donahue, H. M. Newhall and Charles Mayne, three of the Directors of the California Southern Railroad Company, named in the Articles of Association hereto attached, and who being by me severally duly sworn, on their oaths do say, that over one thousand dollars for each and every mile of the railroad proposed and mentioned in the said Articles of Association, to wit, the sum of one million five hundred thousand dollars, has actually and in good faith been subscribed to the stock of the company by the persons whose names appear subscribed to the said Articles of Association, and that ten per

4

cent. on said amount so subscribed, namely, the sum of one hundred and fifty thousand dollars, has actually and in good faith been paid to J. L. Willcutt, the Treasurer named and appointed by said subscribers from among their number, and that the said subscribers are all known to said three Directors, and to each of them, to be subscribers to said Articles of Association, and to be the persons so represented.

PETER DONAHUE.
H. M. NEWHALL.
CHAS. MAYNE.

Subscribed and sworn to before me, this }
  21st day of January, A. D. 1870. }

In witness whereof, I have hereunto subscribed my name and affixed my official seal.

[SEAL.]

SAM'L HERMANN,
Notary Public.

(Endorsed.)

California Southern Railroad Co. Articles of Incorporation, January, 1870.

Filed in office of the Secretary of State, January 22d, 1870.

H. L. NICHOLS,
Sec. of State.
By LEW. B. HARRIS,
Deputy.

{ 5 cent Int. Rev. Stamp. }
{   L. B. H. }
{   Jan. 22, '70. }

CERTIFIED LIST OF OFFICERS

OF THE

CALIFORNIA SOUTHERN RAILROAD COMPANY.

I, J. L. Willcutt, Secretary of the Southern Pacific Railroad Company, hereby certify that at a meeting of the Board of Directors, named in the Articles of Association for the Incorporation of a Railroad Company, to be known as the "California Southern Railroad Company," which meeting was held in the city of San Francisco, on the 21st day of January, A. D. 1870, for the purpose of electing the necessary officers, as prescribed by Statute, the following named persons were duly and legally elected officers of said Company, to serve for the ensuing year:

CHARLES MAYNE was elected President,
MYLES D. SWEENY was elected Treasurer,
J. L. WILLCUTT was elected Secretary,

as appears of record on the minutes of proceedings of the Board of Directors of said California Southern Railroad Company.

[SEAL.] In witness whereof, I have hereunto set my hand and affixed the corporate seal of the Company, this twelfth day of April, A. D. 1871.

J. L. WILLCUTT,
Secretary,
S. P. R. R. Co.

RESOLUTION

OF THE

CALIFORNIA SOUTHERN RAILROAD COMPANY TO CONSOLIDATE WITH OTHER COMPANIES.

At a meeting of the Board of Directors of the California Southern Railroad Company, regularly called and held at the Company's office, in the city and county of San Francisco, on the 11th day of October, A. D. 1870, at which meeting the full Board of Directors were present, to wit:

CHARLES MAYNE,   PETER DONAHUE,
H. M. NEWHALL,   MYLES D. SWEENY,
and RICHARD P. HAMMOND.

The following resolution was offered and adopted by the unanimous vote and concurrence of the full Board of Directors:

Resolved, That this corporation do consolidate with The San Francisco and San José Railroad Company, the Santa Clara

and Pajaro Valley Railroad ʼ Company and the Southern
Pacific Railroad Company, upon the terms and conditions set
forth in the Articles of Association, Amalgamation and Consolidation now herewith presented, which are hereby approved,
and the President and Secretary of this Company are hereby
authorized and required to subscribe the name of this corporation to said articles, and to affix its corporate seal thereto, and
deliver said articles as the Act and deed of this corporation,
and that either face of the half dollar coin of the United States
of America be adopted and used as the seal of this corporation.
The articles referred to in this resolution being as follows, to
wit : (Articles of Association, Amalgamation and Consolidation,
as per accompanying certified copy.)

[SEAL.]
In witness whereof, I have hereunto set my hand
and affixed the corporate seal of the Company,
this twelfth day of April, A. D. 1871.

J. L. WILLCUTT,
Secy: S. P. R. R. Co.

V.

SOUTHERN PACIFIC RAILROAD COMPANY.

(*New Organization.*)

CERTIFIED COPY, ARTICLES OF ASSOCIATION, AMALGAMATION AND
CONSOLIDATION OF

The San Francisco and San José Railroad Company, the
Santa Clara and Pajaro Valley Railroad Company, the South-
ern Pacific Railroad Company, and the California Southern
Railroad Company.

STATE OF CALIFORNIA, }
Department of State. }

{ L. B. H.
Five cent Int. Rev. Stamp.
April 10, 71. }
I, H. L. Nichols, Secretary of State of the
State of California, do hereby certify that
the annexed is a true, full and correct copy of Articles of

Association, Amalgamation and Consolidation, of the Southern
Pacific Railroad Company, with endorsements thereon, now on
file in my office.

Witness my hand and the great seal of State, at
{Seal of State.} office in Sacramento, California, the tenth day of
April, A. D. 1871.

H. L. NICHOLS,
Secretary of State.
By LEW. B. HARRIS,
Deputy.

ARTICLES OF
ASSOCIATION AMALGAMATION AND CONSOLIDATION.

Made and executed on this the eleventh day of October, A. D.
1870, by and between the San Francisco and San José Rail-
road Company, of the first part, the Santa Clara and Pajaro
Valley Railroad Company, of the second part, the Southern
Pacific Railroad Company, of the third part, and the California
Southern Railroad Company, of the fourth part.

WITNESSETH, that whereas the said party of the first part,
was heretofore, to wit, on the eighteenth day of August, 1860,
duly incorporated and organized under the laws of the State
of California, for the purpose of constructing, owning, maintaining and operating a railroad from the city of San Franciso,
in the county of San Francisco, in said State, through said
county, and the counties of San Mateo and Santa Clara, to the
city of San José, in said last named county, a distance of forty-
eight miles.

{5 cent.
Int. Rev.
Stamp.}

And whereas, the said party of the second part was heretofore, to wit, on the second day of January, 1868, duly incorporated and organized under the laws of said State, for the purpose of owning, constructing, maintaining and operating a
railroad from a point at or near the city of San José, in the

county of Santa Clara and State aforesaid, connecting at said point with the railroad of the said party of the first part, and to pass thence to a point at or near the town of New Gilroy, in the same county, a distance of thirty miles.

{ 5 cent.
Int. Rev.
Stamp. }

And whereas, the said party of the third part was heretofore, to wit, on the second day of December, 1865, duly incorporated and organized under the laws of said State, for the purpose of constructing, owning, maintaining and operating a railroad from some point on the Bay of San Francisco, in said State, and to pass through the counties of Santa Clara, Monterey, San Luis Obispo, Tulare, Kern, Los Angeles and San Diego, to the town of San Diego, in said State; thence eastward, through the county of San Diego, to the eastern boundary line of said State, a distance of seven hundred and twenty miles, as near as may be, there to connect with a contemplated railroad from said eastern boundary line of said State to the Mississippi river, and has received large grants of land from the Government of the United States, to aid it in the construction and equipment of said road.

And whereas, the said party of the fourth part, was heretofore, to wit, on the twenty-second day of January, 1870, duly incorporated and organized, under the laws of said State, for the purpose of constructing, owning and maintaining a railroad from a point at or near the town of Gilroy, in the county of Santa Clara, in said State, and to pass through the counties of Santa Clara, Santa Cruz and Monterey, to a point at or near the town of Salinas City, in said last named county, a distance of forty-five miles, as near as may be.

And whereas, said parties believe a consolidation and amalgamation of their capital stocks, debts, properties, assets, roads, telegraphs, lands and franchises will be mutually advantageous.

And whereas, more than three-fourths in value of all the stockholders in interest of each of said parties have consented, in writing, to such amalgamation and consolidation, upon the terms and conditions hereinafter set forth.

{ 5 cent
Int. Rev.
Stamp. }

Now, therefore, under and by virtue ⌐of the statute of the State of California, in such case made and provided, the said parties do hereby mutually covenant and agree, each with each and all the others, to the following articles, to wit:

Article 1. Said parties do hereby amalgamate and consolidate themselves into a new corporation, under the name and style of the Southern Pacific Railroad Company, which new corporation shall continue in existence for the period of fifty years from the date of these articles; and they do further consolidate and amalgamate their several 'capital stocks, debts, properties, assets, roads, telegraphs, lands, franchises, rights, titles, privileges, claims and demands of every kind whatsoever, as well in possession as in expectancy, at law or in equity, and do grant, convey and vest the same in said new corporation as fully as the same are now severally held and enjoyed by them or either of them; subject however, to all conditions, obligations, stipulations, contracts, agreements, liens, mortgages, incumbrances, claims and charges thereon, or in anywise affecting the same.

Article 2. The object and purpose of said new corporation shall be to purchase, construct, own, maintain, and operate a continuous line of railroad, from the city of San Francisco, in the State of California, through the city and county of San Francisco, the counties of San Mateo, Santa Clara, Monterey, Fresno, Tulare, Kern, San Bernadino and San Diego, to some point on the Colorado river, in the southeastern part of the State of California, a distance of seven hundred and twenty miles, as near as may be; also a line of railroad from the town of Gilroy, in the county of Santa Clara, in said State, passing through said county and the counties of Santa Cruz and Monterey, to a point at or near Salinas City, in said last named county, a distance of forty-five miles, as near as may be; also such branches to said lines as the Board of Directors of said new corporation may hereafter consider advantageous to said corporation, and direct to be established.

Article 3. The Board of Directors of said new corporation shall consist of seven persons, and the following named persons shall act as such directors until their successors shall have been duly elected, pursuant to the by-laws of said new corporation hereafter to be adopted, viz.: Lloyd Tevis, Leland Stanford, Charles Crocker, C. P. Huntington, Mark Hopkins, Charles Mayne and Peter Donahue.

Article 4. The capital stock of said new corporation shall be fifty million dollars, consisting of five hundred thousand shares of one hundred dollars each, that sum being the contemplated actual cost of said railroads, including telegraph lines, rolling-stock, motive power, shops, depots, etc.

Article 5. Each stockholder of each of said parties shall have the same number of shares of the capital stock of the new corporation which he now owns and holds of the capital stock of his respective company, upon the same terms and conditions, and shall be entitled to receive from said new corporation certificates therefor, where the same has been fully paid up, upon the surrender of the certificates now held by him, and where the same has not been fully paid up, he shall receive such other evidence of his ownership as the Board of Directors of said new corporation shall direct, upon the surrender of such evidence of his ownership of such unpaid stock of his respective company as he may now hold.

Article 6. Said new corporation shall assume and perform all the contracts, agreements, covenants, duties and obligations, of what kind soever, of each of said parties, and shall pay and discharge all debts, claims and demands existing against either and all of said parties; but nothing herein contained shall release the said parties or either of them, or their stockholders or any of them, from any of their just liabilities.

In testimony whereof, the said parties have severally caused these articles to be signed and executed, by affixing thereto their respective corporate names and seals, by their respective Presidents and Secretaries, pursuant to the orders of their respective Boards of Directors heretofore made, on the day and year first above written.

SOUTHERN PACIFIC RAILROAD CO.
[SEAL.]   By LLOYD TEVIS, President,
B. B. MINOR, Secretary.
THE SAN FRANCISCO & SAN JOSÉ RAILROAD CO.
[SEAL.]   By H. M. NEWHALL, President,
J. L. WILLCUTT, Secretary.
SANTA CLARA & PAJARO VALLEY RAILROAD CO.,
[SEAL.]   ·   By PETER DONAHUE, President,
J. L. WILLCUTT, Secretary.
CALIFORNIA SOUTHERN RAILROAD CO.,
[SEAL.]   By CHARLES MAYNE, President,
J. L. WILLCUTT, Secretary.

{ 5 cent
  Int. Rev.
  Stamp. }

The undersigned, being holders of more than three-fourths in value of the capital stock of the San Francisco & San José Railroad Company, party of the first part, in and to the foregoing articles, do hereby consent to the terms and conditions in said articles contained, and do consent to the consolidation therein provided for.

Done this the eleventh day of October, 1870.

H. M. NEWHALL,	P. DONAHUE,
CHAS. MAYNE,	W. C. RALSTON,
JAS. O'NEILL,	G. PALACHE,
	MYLES D. SWEENY.

{ 5 cent.
  Int. Rev.
  Stamp. }

The undersigned, being holders of more than three-fourths in value of the capital stock of the Santa Clara & Pajaro Valley Railroad Company, party of the second part, in and to the foregoing articles, do hereby consent to the terms and conditions in said articles contained, and do consent to the consolidation therein provided for.

Done this the eleventh day of October, 1870.

H. M. NEWHALL,	P. DONAHUE,
CHAS. MAYNE,	JAS. O'NEILL,
MYLES D. SWEENY,	RICHD. P. HAMMOND,
J. L. WILLCUTT,	J. O. ELDRIDGE,
	EDWARD MARTIN.

{ 5 cent.
  Int. Rev.
  Stamp. }

5

The undersigned, being holders of more than three-fourths in value of the capital stock of the Southern Pacific Railroad Company, party of the third part, in and to the foregoing articles, do hereby consent to the terms and conditions in said articles contained, and do consent to the consolidation therein provided for.

Done this the eleventh day of October, 1870.

LLOYD TEVIS,	THOMAS BELL,
WM. E. BARRON,	W. B. CARR,
by his Atty. in fact	
THOMAS BELL,	B. B. MINOR.

{ 5 cent.
Int. Rev.
Stamp. }

The undersigned, being holders of more than three-fourths in value of the capital stock of the California Southern Railroad Company, party of the fourth part, in and to the foregoing articles, do hereby consent to the terms and conditions in said articles contained, and do consent to the consolidation therein provided for.

Done this the eleventh day of October, 1870.

H. M. NEWHALL,	RICHD. P. HAMMOND,
P. DONAHUE,	J. L. WILLCUTT,
CHAS. MAYNE,	G. PALACHE,
MYLES D. SWEENY,	J. O. ELDRIDGE,
	EDWARD MARTIN.

{ 5 cent.
Int. Rev.
Stamp. }

Endorsed.—

Southern Pacific Railroad Company, being Articles of Association, Amalgamation and Consolidation, of the San Francisco & San José, the Santa Clara & Pajaro Valley Railroad Compy's, and the Southern Pacific and the California Southern R. R. Companies.

Filed in office of the Secretary of State, October 12th, A. D., 1870.

H. L. NICHOLS,
Sec. of St.

VI.

SOUTHERN PACIFIC RAILROAD COMPANY.

CERTIFICATE OF PUBLICATION OF NOTICE OF CONSOLIDATION.

I, J. L. Willcutt, Secretary of the *Southern Pacific Railroad Company,* hereby certify that due notice has been given of the consolidation and amalgamation of the *Southern Pacific Railroad Company, The San Francisco and San José Railroad Company, The Santa Clara and Pajaro Valley Railroad Company,* and the *California Southern Railroad Company,* by advertising the same, pursuant to section forty (40) of the General Railroad Law of California.

The annexed is a copy of said notice, and the following are the names of papers in which the same has been published, as per affidavits of publication on file in my office.

RAILROAD CONSOLIDATION.

Pursuant to the statute in such case made and provided, notice is hereby given that the Southern Pacific Railroad Company, The San Francisco & San José Railroad Company, the Santa Clara & Pajaro Valley Railroad Company and the California Southern Railroad Company, upon the written consent of the stockholders holding more than three-fourths of the capital stock of each of said corporations respectively, and by the agreement of the respective Boards of Directors of said corporations, made and entered into in accordance with such consent, and pursuant to the statute in such case made and provided, have, this day, amalgamated and consolidated their capital stock, debts, property, assets and franchises under the corporate name and style of the Southern Pacific Railroad Company. By order of the Board of Directors of the Southern Pacific Railroad Company.

J. L. WILLCUTT,
Secretary.

SAN. FRANCISCO, October 12, 1870.

oc. 13, 1 m.

NAMES.	WHERE PUBLISHED.
San Mateo Co. Gazette	Redwood City, San Mateo county.
Santa Clara Argus. . . .	San José, Santa Clara county.
Salinas Standard	Salinas City, Monterey county.
Fresno Expositor	Millerton, Fresno county.
Tulare Times.	Visalia, Tulare county.
Kern County Weekly Courier.	Bakersfield, Kern county.
Guardian.	San Bernadino, San Bernadino county.
San Diego Union.	San Diego, San Diego county.
Sacramento Record. . .	Sacramento, Sacramento county.
Daily Alta California.	San Francisco, San Francisco county.
Daily Evening Bulletin	Do. do. do.

In witness whereof, I have hereunto set my hand,
[SEAL.]   and affixed the corporate seal of the Company,
this 13th day of April, A. D. 1871.

J. L. WILLCUTT,
Secy. So. Pacific R. R. Co.

VII.

SOUTHERN PACIFIC RAILROAD COMPANY.

CERTIFIED COPY OF AMENDED CERTIFICATE OF INCORPORATION.

STATE OF CALIFORNIA, }
Department of State. }

{ L. B. H. 5 ct. Int. Rev. Stamp. April 15, 1871. }   I, H. L. Nichols, Secretary of State for the State of California, do hereby certify that the annexed is a true, full and correct copy of the amended Certificate of Incorporation of the Southern Pacific Railroad Company, now on file in my office.

> Witness my hand and the great seal of State, at office in Sacramento, California, the 15th day of April, A. D. 1871.

{Seal of State.}

H. L. NICHOLS,
Secretary of State.
By LEW. B. HARRIS,
Deputy.

AMENDED CERTIFICATE OF INCORPORATION OF THE SOUTHERN PACIFIC RAILROAD COMPANY.

Whereas, by an Act of the Legislature of the State of California, entitled "An Act relating to Certificates of Incorporation," approved March 1, 1870, any corporation then organized, or thereafter to be organized, under the laws of the State of California, is authorized and empowered to amend its articles of association, or certificate of incorporation, by a majority vote of the Board of Directors or Trustees, and by a vote or written assent of the stockholders representing, at least, two-thirds of the capital stock of such corporation.

And whereas, by a certain other Act of the Legislature of the State of California, entitled "An Act to aid in giving effect to an Act of Congress, relating to the Southern Pacific Railroad Company," approved April 4, 1870, to enable the said company to more fully and completely comply with and perform the provisions, requirements and conditions of an Act of Congress of the United States of America, entitled "An Act granting lands to aid in the construction of a railroad and telegraph line from San Francisco to the eastern line of the State of California," approved July 27, 1866, and of all other Acts of Congress then in force, or which might thereafter be enacted, the said Southern Pacific Railroad Company, its successors and assigns, were authorized and empowered to change the line of its railroad, so as to reach the eastern boundary line of the State of California by such route as said company might determine to be most practicable, and to file new and amendatory Articles of Association.

And whereas, by an Act of Congress of the United States of America, entitled "An Act to incorporate Texas Pacific Railroad Company and aid in the construction of its road, and for other purposes," approved March 3d, 1871.

The said Southern Pacific Railroad Company was authorized, subject to the laws of California, to construct a line of railroad from a point at, or near Taheechaypah pass, by way of Los Angeles to the Texas Pacific Railroad, at or near the Colorado river, with the same grants, rights and privileges, and subject to the same limitations, restrictions and conditions as were granted to said Southern Pacific Railroad Company by an Act of Congress, entitled "An Act granting lands to aid in the construction of a railroad and telegraph line, from the States of Missouri and Arkansas to the Pacific coast," approved July 27, 1866.

And whereas, said Southern Pacific Railroad Company desires to secure to itself the grants, rights and privileges conferred upon it by said Acts of the Congress of the United States, and to that end to amend and alter its articles of association, as provided in the foregoing Acts of the Legislature of the State of California, so as to include in its line of railroad and telegraph, the line or route designated in the aforesaid Act of Congress of March 3d, 1871, to wit : The line from a point at or near Taheechaypah pass, by way of Los Angeles, to the Texas Pacific Railroad, at or near the Colorado river.

And whereas, on the 11th day of April, 1871, at a meeting of the Board of Directors of said company, held at San Francisco, the principal place of business of said company, it was determined by a unanimous vote of said Board, that the articles of association of said Company be amended as aforesaid.

And whereas, at the same time and place, at a meeting of the stockholders of said company, at which stockholders of said company holding more than two-thirds of the capital stock of said company were present, and did vote unanimously in favor of amending the articles of association of said company as aforesaid, and did also unanimously vote to increase the capital stock of said company to the sum of seventy millions of dollars, to meet the increased cost of the construction and equipment of said railroad.

Now, therefore, the Board of Directors of said Southern Pacific Railroad, do order and direct that the articles of association of said company be amended so as to read as follows:

ARTICLES OF ASSOCIATION, AMALGAMATION AND CONSOLIDATION.

Made and executed on this the eleventh day of October, A. D. 1870, by and between the San Francisco & San José Railroad Company of the first part, the Santa Clara & Pajaro Valley Railroad Company of the second part, the Southern Pacific Railroad Company of the third part, and the California Southern Railroad Company of the fourth part, witnesseth:

That whereas, the said party of the first part was heretofore, to wit, on the eighteenth day of August, 1860, duly incorporated and organized under the laws of the State of California, for the purpose of constructing, owning, maintaining and operating a railroad from the city of San Francisco, in the county of San Francisco, in said State, through said county and the counties of San Mateo and Santa Clara, to the city of San José, in said last named county, a distance of forty-eight miles.

And whereas, the said party of the second part was heretofore, to wit, on the second day of January, 1868, duly incorporated and organized under the laws of said State, for the purpose of "constructing, owning, maintaining" and operating a railroad from a point at or near the city of San Jose, in the county of Santa Clara and State aforesaid, connecting at said point with the railroad of the said party of the first part, and to pass thence to a point at or near the town of New Gilroy, in the same county, a distance of thirty miles.

And whereas, the said party of the third part was heretofore, to wit, on the second day of December 1865, duly incorporated and organized under the laws of said State, for the purpose of constructing, owning, maintaining and operating a railroad, from some point on the bay of San Francisco, in said State, and to pass through the counties of Santa Clara, Monterey, San Luis Obispo, Tulare, Kern, Los Angeles and San Diego, to the town of San Diego, in said State; thence eastward through the county of San Diego to the eastern boundary line of said State, a distance of seven hundred and twenty miles as near as may be, there to connect with a contemplated railroad from said eastern boundary line of said State to the Mississippi river, and has received large grants of land from the Government of the United States to aid it in the construction and equipment of said road.

And whereas, the said party of the fourth part was heretofore, to wit, on the twenty-second day of January, 1870, duly incorporated and organized under the laws of said State, for the purpose of constructing, owning and maintaining a railroad from a point at or near the town of Gilroy, in the county of Santa Clara, in said State, and to pass through the counties of Santa Clara, Santa Cruz and Monterey, to a point at or near the town of Salinas City, in said last named county, a distance of forty-five miles, as near as may be.

And whereas, said parties believe a consolidation and amalgamation of their capital stocks, debts, properties, assets, roads, telegraphs, lands and franchises, will be mutually advantageous.

And whereas, more than three-fourths in value of all the stockholders in interest of each of said parties have consented, in writing, to such amalgamation and consolidation, upon the terms and conditions hereinafter set forth.

Now, therefore, under and by virtue of the statute of the State of California, in such case made and provided, the said parties do hereby mutually covenant and agree, each with each and all the others, to the following articles, to wit:

Article 1. Said parties do hereby amalgamate and consolidate themselves into a new corporation, under the name and style of the Southern Pacific Railroad Company, which new corporation shall continue in existence for the period of fifty years from the date of these articles ; and they do further consolidate and amalgamate their several capital stocks, debts, properties, assets, roads, telegraphs, lands, franchises, rights, titles, privileges, claims and demands of every kind whatsoever, as well in possession as in expectancy, at law or in equity. and do grant, convey and vest the same in said new corporation, as fully as the same are now severally held and enjoyed by them, or either of them, subject, however, to all conditions, obligations, stipulations, contracts, agreements, liens, mortgages, encumbrances, claims and charges thereon, or in anywise af. fecting the same.

Article 2. The object and purpose of said new corporation shall be to purchase, construct, own, maintain and operate a continuous line of railroad from the city of San Francisco, in the State of California, through the city and county of San Francisco, the counties of San Mateo, Santa Clara, Monterey, Fresno, Tulare, Kern, San Bernadino and San Diego, to some point on the Colorado river, in the south-eastern part of the State of California, a distance of seven hundred and twenty miles, as near as may be ; also a line of railroad from a point at or near Tahecchaypah pass, by way of Los Angeles, to the Texas Pacific Railroad, at or near the Colorado river, a distance of three hundred and twenty-four miles, as near as may be ; also a line of railroad from the town of Gilroy, in the county of Santa Clara, in said State, passing through said county and the counties of Santa Cruz and Monterey, to a point at or near Salinas City, in said last named county, a distance of forty-five miles, as near as may be ; also such branches to said lines as the Board of Directors of said new corporation may hereafter consider advantageous to said corporation, and direct to be established.

Article 3. The Board of Directors of said new corporation shall consist of seven persons, and the following named persons shall act as such directors until their successors shall have been duly elected, pursuant to the by-laws of said new corporation, hereafter to be adopted, viz.: Lloyd Tevis, Leland

6

Stanford, Charles Crocker, C. P. Huntington, Mark Hopkins, Charles Mayne and Peter Donahue.

Article 4. The capital stock of said new corporation shall be seventy million dollars, consisting of seven hundred thousand shares, of one hundred dollars each, that sum being the contemplated actual cost of said railroads, including telegraph lines, rolling stock, motive power, shops, depots, &c.

Article 5. Each stockholder of each of said parties shall have the same number of shares of the capital stock of the new corporation which he now owns and holds of the capital stock of his respective company, upon the same terms and conditions, and shall be entitled to receive from said new corporation certificates therefor, where the same has been fully paid up, upon the surrender of the certificates now held by him, and where the same has not been fully paid up, he shall receive such other evidence of his ownership as the Board of Directors of said new corporation shall direct, upon the surrender of such evidence of his ownership of such unpaid stock of his respective company as he may now hold.

Article 6. Said new corporation shall assume and perform all the contracts, agreements, covenants, duties and obligations, of what kind soever, of each of said parties, and shall pay and discharge all debts, claims and demands existing against either and all of said parties, but nothing herein contained shall release the said parties or either of them, or their stockholders or any of them, from any of their just liabilities.

In testimony whereof, the said Southern Pacific Railroad Company, by its Board of Directors, has caused these articles to be signed and countersigned by its President and Secretary, and its corporate seal to be hereunto affixed, on this, the eleventh (11) day of April, 1871.

SOUTHERN PACIFIC RAILROAD COMPANY,

By CHARLES CROCKER,

President.

[SEAL].

J. L. WILLCUTT,

Secretary.

Endorsed—

    Southern Pacific R. R. Co. Amended Certificate of Incorporation, filed in office of the Secretary of State, April, 15, 1871.

H. L. NICHOLS,
Secretary of State.

By LEW. B. HARRIS,
Deputy.

BY-LAWS

OF THE

SOUTHERN PACIFIC RAILROAD COMPANY.

SECTION 1. The annual meeting of the stockholders of this Company shall be held at the principal place of business of the Company on the second Monday of August in each year, or at such other time as shall be appointed by a resolution of the Board of Directors, at which an election for seven Directors shall be held, to serve for the ensuing year, and until their successors are elected. Said election shall commence and terminate at hours designated by the Board of Directors and named in the notice calling the meeting. *Annual meetings of Stockholders. Place. Time of. Election of Directors. Time of Election.*

SECTION 2. The President, or in his absence the Vice-President of the Company, together with one Director, and one stockholder who is not at the time a Director, both to be chosen and appointed by the Board of Directors for that purpose, shall act as the Judges of Election, receive, count and canvass the votes, and declare the result without delay. The Secretary shall be tally clerk, and shall keep a regular tally list of all votes cast at said election and preserve the same in his office. The vote for the election of Directors shall be taken by ballot, and each voter shall indorse on his ballot his name and the number of votes cast by him. The said Judges of Election and Secretary shall, at the close of such election, certify the result thereof to the Board of Directors. In the *Elections. Officers to preside. Judges of election. Tally Clerk. Voters and number of votes. Vote by ballot. Election of Directors.*

absence of any officer of election, his place shall be filled by the stockholders present at the opening of the election.

Meetings of Stockholders.
Who to vote.
List of voters.

SECTION 3. At all meetings of the stockholders, absent members may vote by proxy duly authorized in writing, signed by the stockholder granting them, and they shall be filed with the Secretary. It shall be the duty of the Secretary, previous to every meeting thereof, to make an alphabetical list of all stockholders, with the number of votes each is entitled to cast set opposite his or her name, and have the same present at such meeting for the use of the officers thereof.

Office of the Company.
Fiscal year.

SECTION 4. The office of the Company and of the President, Secretary, Treasurer and Chief Engineer, with the books and papers thereto belonging, shall be kept in the city of San Francisco. The fiscal year of the Company shall commence on the first day of July and terminate on the last day of June in each year, and shall be divided into four quarters, terminating on the last days of September, December, March and June, respectively.

Directors' meetings.
Quorum.
Special meetings.

SECTION 5. The regular monthly meetings of the Board of Directors shall be held on the second Tuesday of each month, at two o'clock in the afternoon, at the office of the Company, unless otherwise specially directed by the Board, and four or more of the Directors shall constitute a quorum at all meetings for the transaction of business. Special meetings may at any time be called by the President, or any three members of the Board, to convene at such time and place as may be appointed, but it shall require a majority of the whole Board to adopt any measure.

Election of Officers by Directors.
Term of Office.

SECTION 6. There shall be elected by the Directors at their first meeting after the annual election of Directors, which shall be within five days thereafter, or at such subsequent meeting of the Board as said election may be adjourned to, from among their number a President, a Vice-President, and a Treasurer, and also a Secretary, who need not necessarily be a Director, who shall hold their offices for the term of one year, and until their successors are elected and qualified, unless previously removed, and who shall receive such salaries as may be allowed by the Board of Directors.

Section 7. The Secretary of the Company shall perform *Secretary—his duties.* the duties prescribed by Statutes, and shall make out a quarterly and an annual statement and balance sheet at the end of each quarter and year, up to and including the last days of each of said quarters and year, showing the financial condition of the Company at each of said periods, and lay the same before the Board at the next regular meeting after the expiration of said quarter and year, and perform such other official duties as may be required of him by the Board of Directors.

Section 8. Certificates of Stock shall be issued only for fully *Stock Certificates.* paid stock, and shall be of such form and device as the Board *When issued.* of Directors shall determine, and each certificate shall be signed *Form.* by the President and Secretary, and express on its face its *How signed.* number, date of issue, the number of shares for which, and the *What to contain.* name of the person to whom, it is issued. The certificate book shall contain a margin, on which shall be entered the number, *Certificate Book.* date, number of shares, and the name of the shareholder expressed in the corresponding certificate. The surrendered *Entry in.* certificate shall in all cases be canceled by the Secretary before issuing a new one in lieu thereof. In all cases where a certificate of stock shall have been issued, no transfer of such stock shall be made on the "Stock Transfer Book" until such cer- *Certificates. to be returned.* tificates shall have been returned to the Company, and in case of the alleged loss or destruction of a certificate of stock, due *Loss of Certificate.* proof of such loss or destruction shall be made, and a sufficient *Proof of loss.* bond of indemnity against any loss or damage the Company *Indemnity.* may sustain should said certificate afterwards reappear, shall be executed to the Company, and approved by the Board of Directors, before a duplicate thereof shall be issued, and before any transfer of such stock shall be entered on the Stock Transfer Book.

Section 9. These By-Laws may be amended or suspended at any time by the Board of Directors.

ACTS OF CONGRESS

RELATIVE TO THE

SOUTHERN PACIFIC RAILROAD COMPANY.

ATLANTIC AND PACIFIC RAILROAD COMPANY'S CHARTER.

[Approved July 27, 1866.]

(14 U. S. Statutes at Large, page 292.)

Chap. CCLXXVII.

An Act Granting Lands to Aid in the Construction of a Railroad and Telegraph Line from the States of Missouri and Arkansas to the Pacific Coast.

Be it enacted by the Senate and House of Representatives of the United States of America, in Congress assembled, that John B. Brown, Anson P. Morrill, Samuel F. Hersey, William G. Crosby, Samuel E. Spring, Samuel P. Dinsmore, of Maine ; N. S. Upham, Frederick Smyth, Onslow Stearns, S. G. Griffin, William E. Chandler, of New Hampshire; T. W. Parke, H. H. Baxter, John

Atlantic and Pacific Railroad Company incorporated.

7

Gregory Smith, A. P. Lyman, of Vermont; Walter S. Burges, William S. Slater, Stephen Harris, Thomas P. Shepard, of Rhode Island; William Merritt, Alexander H. Bullock, George L. Stearns, Genery Twitchell, Charles H. Warren, Chester W. Chapin, of Massachusetts; John Boyd, Robert C. Wetmore, John T. Wait, Cyrus Northrop, of Connecticut; Solon Humphreys, J. Bigler, Homer Ramsdell, Isaac H. Knox, John A. C. Gray, Daniel L. Ross, A. V. Stout, M. K. Jessup, R. E. Fenton, E. L. Fancher, J. C. Fremont, James Hoy, Jesse M. Bolles, Edward Gilbert, James P. Robinson, Oliver C. Billings, of New York; Charles Bachelor, John Edgar Thompson, Morton McMichael, T. Haskins Du Puy, Thomas A. Scott, Charles Rickettson, William Lyon, George W. Cass, Levi Parsons, of Pennsylvania; Charles Knap, J. L. N. Stratton, James B. Dayton, Robert F. Stockton, Alexander G. Cattell, A. W. Markley, of New Jersey; John W. Garrett, Charles J. M. Gwinn, Robert Fowler, Jacob Tome, Thomas M. Lanahan, of Maryland; Charles J. Dupont, Henry Ridgely, Andrew C. Gray, Nat. Smythers, of Delaware; Bellamy Storer, George B. Senter, William Baker, Samuel Galloway, David Tod, Charles Anderson. Bird B. Chapman, Edward Sturgis, Israel Dille, of Ohio; Edwin Peck, William D. Griswold, James P. Luse, Samuel E. Perkins, Conrad Baker, of Indiana; Richard J. Oglesby, N. B. Judd, Samuel A. Buckmaster, D. L. Phillips, L. P. Sanger, of Illinois; Eber B. Ward, Omar D. Congar, Nathaniel W. Brooks, Alexander H. Morrison, of Michigan; Z. G. Simmons, Alexander Mitchell, J. J. Williams, G. A. Thompson, J. J. R. Pease, John H. Hersey, of Wisconsin; Henry A. Smith, Sherman Finch, William Mitchell, R. F. Crowell, L. F. Hubbard, E. F. Drake, of Minnesota; Lyman Cook, Platt Smith, Jacob Butler, Henry I. Reid, Hoyt Sherman, of Iowa; William G. Brownlow, of Tennessee; Thomas C. Fletcher, B. R. Bonner, John M. Richardson, Emil Pretorious, E. W. Fox, R. J. McElheny, Charles H. Howland, Madison Miller, George W. Fishback, T. J. Hubbard, George Knapp, Charles K. Dickson, A. G. Braun, G. L. Hewitt, P. A. Thompson, James W. Thomas, Charles E. Moss, Edward Walsh, A. R. Easton, Truman J. Horner, J. B. Eads, D. R. Garrison, W. A. Kayser, George P. Robinson, of Missouri; Thomas E. Bramlette, Benjamin Gratz, C. E. Warren, Lazarus W. Powell, John Mason Brown, Joshua Speed, of Kentucky; Solon Thatcher, Jacob Stotter, William B. Edwards, James G. Blunt, Robert McBratney, of Kansas; Harrison Hagans, James Cook, Robert Crangle, Benjamin H. Smith, of West Virginia; Lorenzo Sherwood, A. J. Hamilton, of

Texas; William Gilpin, Henry C. Leach, of Colorado; Phineas Banning, Timothy G. Phelps, William B. Carr, Edward F. Beale, Fred. F. Low, Benj. B. Redding, B. W. Hathaway, Leonidas Haskell, Frederick Billings, of California; W. S. Ladd, J. R. Moores, Walter Monteith, John Kelley, B. F. Dowell, of Oregon; James L. Johnson, Henry Connelly, Franciscus Perea, of New Mexico; J. H. Mills, A. P. K. Safford, E. S. Davis, of Nevada; King S. Woolsey, William H. Hardy, Coles Bashford, of Arizona; Henry D. Cooke, of the District of Columbia; and all such other persons who shall or may be associated with them, and their successors, are hereby created and erected into a body corporate and politic, in deed and in law, by the name, style, and title of the "Atlantic and Pacific **Name of Corporation, &c.** Railroad Company," and by that name shall have perpetual succession, and shall be able to sue and be sued, plead and be impleaded, defend and be defended, in all Courts of law and equity within the United States, and may make and have a common seal. And **Seal.** said corporation is hereby authorized and empowered to lay out, locate and construct, furnish, maintain and enjoy a continuous railroad and telegraph line, with the appurtenances, namely: Begining at or near the town of Springfield, in the State of Missouri, thence to the western boundary line of said State, and thence **Corporation may locate and** by the most eligible railroad route as shall be determined by said **construct railroad and tele-** company, to a point on the Canadian river, thence to the town of **graph line.** Albuquerque, on the River del Norte, and thence by way of the Agua Frio, or other suitable pass, to the head-waters of the Colora- **Termini and** do Chiquito, and thence along the thirty-fifth parallel of latitude, **route.** as near as may be found most suitable for a railway route, to the Colorado river, at such point as may be selected by said company for crossing; thence by the most practicable and eligible route to the Pacific. The said company shall have the right to construct a **Branch east-** branch from the point at which the road strikes the Canadian river **wardly near to** eastwardly, along the most suitable route as selected, to a point in **Van Buren, Ar-** the western boundary line of Arkansas, at or near the town of **kansas.** Van Buren. And the said company is hereby vested with all the **Powers and** powers, privileges and immunities necessary to carry into effect **privileges.** the purposes of this act, as herein set forth. The capital stock of **Capital stock.** said company shall consist of one million shares of one hundred dollars each, which shall in all respects be deemed personal property, and shall be transferable in such manner as the laws of said corporation shall provide. The persons hereinbefore named **Persons be-** are hereby appointed commissioners, and shall be called the Board **fore named appointed Board of**

Commissioners. of Commissioners of the "Atlantic and Pacific Railroad Company,"

Quorum. and fifteen shall constitute a quorum for the transaction of busi-

First meeting of Commission-ers. ness. The first meeting of said board of commissioners shall be held at the Turner Hall, in the city of St. Louis, on the first day of October, anno Domini eighteen hundred and sixty-six, or at such time within three months thereafter as any ten commissioners

Notice. herein named from Missouri shall appoint, notice of which shall be given by them to the other commissioners by publishing said notice in at least one daily newspaper in the cities of Boston, New York, Cincinnati, Saint Louis, Memphis and Nashville, once a week, for

Organization of board and officers. at least four weeks previous to the day of meeting. Said board shall organize by the choice from its number of a president, vice-president, secretary and treasurer, and they shall require from said

Treasurer to give bonds. treasurer such bonds as may be deemed proper, and may from time to time increase the amount thereof, as they may deem proper.

Secretary to be sworn. The secretary shall be sworn to the faithful performance of his du-ties, and such oath shall be entered upon the records of the com-pany, signed by him, and the oath verified thereon. The president and secretary of said boards shall, in like manner call all other

Other meetings, how called. meetings, naming the time and place thereof. It shall be the duty of said board of commissioners to open books, or cause books to

Commissioners to open books for subscrip-tions to stock. be opened, at such times and in such principal cities or other places in the United States as they or a quorum of them shall determine, within twelve months after the passage of this act, to receive sub-scriptions to the capital stock of said corporation, and a cash pay-ment of ten per centum on all subscriptions, and to receipt there-

When and how first meeting of subscribers to stock to be call-ed. for. So soon as ten thousand shares shall in good faith be sub-scribed for, and ten dollars per share actually paid into the treas-ury of the company, the said president and secretary of said board of commissioners shall appoint a time and place for the first meet-ing of the subscribers to the stock of said company, and shall give notice thereof in at least one newspaper in each State in which subscription books have been opened, at least fifteen days previous to the day of meeting, and such subscribers as shall attend the meet-ing so called, either in person or by lawful proxy, then and there

Directors. shall elect, by ballot, thirteen directors for said corporation; and in such election each share of said capital stock shall entitle the

Each share to have a vote. owner thereof to one vote. The president and secretary of the board of commissioners, and in case of their absence or inability,

Inspectors of Election. any two of the officers of said board, shall act as inspectors of said election, and shall certify, under their hands, the names of the directors elected at said meeting. And the said commissioners, treasurer and secretary shall then deliver over to said directors all the moneys, property, subscription books and other books in their possession, and thereupon the duties of said commissioners and the officers previously appointed by them shall cease and determine forever, and thereafter the stockholders shall constitute said body politic and corporate. Annual meetings of the stockholders of the said corporation for the choice of officers (when they are to be chosen) and for the transaction of business, shall be holden at such time and place, and upon such notice as may be prescribed in the by-laws.

Commissioners to deliver to Directors all moneys, books, &c., and their duties to cease.

Annual meetings of Corporation.

SEC. 2. *And be it further enacted,* That the right of way through the public lands be, and the same is hereby granted to the said Atlantic and Pacific Railroad Company, its successors and assigns, for the construction of a railroad and telegraph as proposed; and the right, power and authority is hereby given to said corporation to take from the public lands adjacent to the line of said road material of earth, stone, timber, and so forth, for the construction thereof. Said way is granted to said railroad to the extent of one hundred feet in width on each side of said railroad where it may pass through the public domain, including all necessary grounds for station buildings, workshops, depots, machine shops, switches, side-tracks, turn-tables and water stations; and the right of way shall be exempt from taxation within the territories of the United States. The United States shall extinguish, as rapidly as may be consistent with public policy and the welfare of the Indians, and only by their voluntary cession, the Indian title to all lands falling under the operation of this act and acquired in the donation to the road named in the act.

Right of way granted through public lands for construction of railroad and telegraph.

Material for construction.

Extent of grant of right of way.

Right of way exempt from taxation.

Indian title to be extinguished

SEC. 3. *And be it further enacted,* That there be, and hereby is granted to the Atlantic and Pacific Railroad Company, its successors and assigns, for the purpose of aiding in the construction of said railroad and telegraph line to the Pacific coast, and to secure the safe and speedy transportation of the mails, troops, munitions of war and public stores, over the route of said line of railway and its branches, every alternate section of public land, not mineral, designated by odd numbers, to the amount of twenty alternate sections per mile, on each side of said railroad line, as said company may adopt, through the Territories of the United States, and ten alternate sections of land per mile on each side of said railroad

Public lands granted to the Corporation to aid in the construction of railroad and telegraph.

whenever it passes through any State, and whenever, on the line thereof, the United States have full title, not reserved, sold, granted, or otherwise appropriated, and free from preëmption or other claims or rights, at the time the line of said road is designated by a plat thereof, filed in the office of the commissioner of the General Land Office, and whenever, prior to said time, any of said sections or parts of sections shall have been granted, sold, reserved, occupied by homestead settlers, or preëmpted, or otherwise disposed of, other lands shall be selected by said company in lieu thereof, under the direction of the Secretary of the Interior, in alternate sections, and designated by odd numbers, not more than ten miles beyond the limits of said alternate sections, and not including the reserved numbers : *Provided*, that if said route shall be found upon the line of any other railroad route, to aid in the construction of which lands have been heretofore granted by the United States, as far as the routes are upon the same general line, the amount of land heretofore granted shall be deducted from the amount granted by this act : *Provided further*, That the railroad company receiving the previous grant of land may assign their interest to said "Atlantic and Pacific Railroad Company," or may consolidate, confederate and associate with said company upon the terms named in the first and seventeenth sections of this act; *Provided further*, That all mineral lands be, and the same are hereby, excluded from the operations of this act, and in lieu thereof a like quantity of unoccupied and unappropriated agricultural lands in odd-numbered sections nearest to the line of said road, and within twenty miles thereof, may be selected as above provided ; *And provided further*, That the word "mineral," when it occurs in this act, shall not be held to include iron or coal; *And provided further*, That no money shall be drawn from the treasury of the United States to aid in the construction of the said "Atlantic and Pacific Railroad."

SEC. 4. *And be it further enacted*, That whenever said Atlantic and Pacific Railroad Company shall have twenty-five consecutive miles of any portion of said railroad and telegraph line ready for the service contemplated, the President of the United States shall appoint three commissioners to examine the same, who shall be paid a reasonable compensation for their services by the company, to be determined by the Secretary of the Interior ; and if it shall appear that twenty-five consecutive miles of said road and tele-

---

Marginal notes:

If any of granted lands have been sold or reserved, &c., other lands may be selected in lieu thereof.

If route is found to be upon the line of any other road to which lands have been granted, amount of former grant to be deducted.

Road having previous grant may assign to, or unite with, this Company.

Mineral lands excluded from operation of this act.

The word "mineral" not to include "iron or coal."

No money to be drawn from treasury to aid in construction of this road.

Upon report of Commissioners, under oath, that twenty-five consecutive miles are completed, patents for co-terminus lands to issue to Company;

graph line have been completed in a good, substantial and work-manlike manner, as in all other respects required by this act, the commissioners shall so report under oath, to the President of the United States, and patents of lands, as aforesaid, shall be issued to said company, confirming to said company the right and title to said lands situated opposite to and coterminous with said completed section of said road. And from time to time, whenever twenty-five additional consecutive miles shall have been constructed, completed, and in readiness as aforesaid, and verified by said commissioners to the President of the United States, then patents shall be issued to said company conveying the additional sections of land as aforesaid, and so on as fast as every twenty-five miles of said road is completed as aforesaid. *And so as to any other twenty-five consecutive miles.*

SEC. 5. *And be it further enacted,* That said Atlantic and Pacific Railroad shall be constructed in a substantial and workmanlike manner, with all the necessary draws, culverts, bridges, viaducts, crossings, turnouts, stations and watering places, and all other appurtenances, including furniture and rolling stock, equal in all respects to railroads of the first class when prepared for business, with rails of the best quality, manufactured from American iron. And a uniform gauge shall be established throughout the entire length of the road. And there shall be constructed a telegraph line, of the most substantial and approved description, to be operated along the entire line; *Provided,* That the said company shall not charge the government higher rates than they do individuals for like transportation and telegraphic service. And it shall be the duty of the Atlantic and Pacific Railroad Company to permit any other railroad which shall be authorized to be built by the United States, or by the Legislature of any Territory or State in which the same may be situated, to form running connections with it, on fair and equitable terms. *Railroad, how to be constructed. Rails. Gauge. Telegraph line, rates for service. Other railroads may form running connections with it.*

SEC. 6. *And be it further enacted,* That the President of the United States shall cause the lands to be surveyed for forty miles in width on both sides of the entire line of said road after the general route shall be fixed, and as fast as may be required by the construction of said railroad; and the odd sections of land hereby granted shall not be liable to sale or entry, or preëmption, before or after they are surveyed, except by said company, as provided in this act; but the provisions of the act of September, eighteen hundred and forty-one, granting preëmption rights, and the acts amendatory thereof, *Lands on both sides of line of route of railroad. Odd sections not liable to sale or entry or preëmption. Provisions of preëmption and homestead* acts extended to lands on line of road, 1841, ch. 16, § 10. Vol. V, p. 455, 1862, ch. 75. Vol. XII, p. 392. and of the act entitled "An act to secure homesteads to actual settlers on the public domain," approved May twenty, eighteen hundred and sixty-two, shall be, and the same are hereby, extended to all other lands on the line of said road when surveyed, excepting those hereby granted to said company.

SEC. 7. *And be it further enacted,* That the said Atlantic and Pacific Railroad Company be, and is hereby, authorized and empowered to enter upon, purchase, take and hold any lands or premises that may be necessary and proper for the construction and working of said road, not exceeding in width one hundred feet on each side of the line of its railroad, unless a greater width be required for the purpose of excavation or embankment; and also any lands or premises that may be necessary and proper for turnouts, standing places for cars, depots, station-houses, or any other structures required in the construction and working of said road And the said company shall have the right to cut and remove trees and other material that might, by falling, encumber its road-bed, though standing or being more than two hundred feet from the line of said road. And in case the owner of such lands or premises and the said company cannot agree as to the value of the premises taken, or to be taken, for the use of said road, the value thereof shall be determined by the appraisal of three disinterested commissioners, who may be appointed upon application by either party to any court of record in any of the Territories in which the lands or premises to be taken lie; and said commissioners, in their assessment of damages, shall appraise such premises at what would have been the value thereof if the road had not been built. And upon return into court of such appraisement. and upon the payment into the same of the estimated value of the premises taken for the use and benefit of the owner thereof, said premises shall be deemed to be taken by said company, which shall thereby acquire full title to the same for the purposes aforesaid. And either party feeling aggrieved at said appraisement may, within thirty days after the same has been returned into court, file an appeal therefrom, and demand a jury of twelve men to estimate the damage sustained; but such appeal shall not interfere with the rights of said company to enter upon the premises taken, or to do any act necessary and proper in the construction of its road. And said party appealing shall give bonds, with sufficient surety or sureties, for the payment of any cost that may arise upon such appeal; and

Marginal notes:
Company may take any land necessary for working of road. Width.

Lands for stations.

Trees.

Damages, how to be determined.

When lands are to be deemed taken by the Company.

Appeal to a jury.

Appellant to give bonds.

in case the party appealing does not obtain a verdict more favorable, such party shall pay the whole cost incurred by the appellee, Costs. as well as his own, and the payment into court, for the use of the Payment into court of a sum owner of said premises taken, at a sum equal to that finally awarded. equal to final award, to vest shall be held to vest in said company the title of said land, and title of land in Company. the right to use and occupy the same for the construction, maintenance and operation of said road. And in case any of the lands to be taken as aforesaid, shall be held by an infant, feme covert, non compos, insane person, or persons residing without the Territory within which the lands to be taken lie, or persons subjected to Proceedings where lands any legal disability, the court may appoint a guardian, for any party taken are held by persons un- under any disqualification, to appear in proper person, who shall der disability. give bonds, with sufficient surety or sureties, for the proper and faithful execution of his trust, and who may represent in court the person disqualified, as aforesaid, from appearing, when the same proceedings shall be had in reference to the appraisement of the premises to be taken for the use of said company, and with the same effect as has been already described; and the title of the company to the lands taken by virtue of this act shall not be affected or impaired by reason of any failure by any guardian to discharge faithfully his trust. And in case any party shall have a right or Proceedings claim to any land for a term of years, or any interest therein, in where the interest in the land possession, reversion or remainder, the value of any such estate is for a term of years, &c.; less than a fee simple, shall be estimated and determined in the where lands are unoccupied and manner hereinbefore set forth. And in case it shall be necessary without appar-ent owner. for the company to enter upon any lands which are unoccupied, and of which there is no apparent owner or claimant, it may proceed to take and use the same for the purposes of said railroad, and may institute proceedings, in manner described, for the purpose of ascertaining the value of, and of acquiring a title to, the same; but the judge of the court hearing said suit shall determine the kinds of notice to be served on such owner or owners, and he may in his discretion appoint an agent or guardian to represent such owner or owners in case of his or their incapacity or non-appearance. But in case no claimant shall appear within six years from the time of the opening of said road across any land, all claims to damages against said company shall be barred.

Sec. 8. *And be it further enacted,* That each and every grant, Rights and right and privilege herein are so made and given to and accepted privileges of this by said Atlantic and Pacific Railroad Company, upon and subject act are granted and accepted, upon conditions &c.

Work, when to be commenced and when completed.
to the following conditions, namely: That the said company shall commence the work on said road within two years from the approval of this act by the President, and shall complete not less than fifty miles per year after the second year, and shall construct, equip, furnish and complete the main line of the whole road by the fourth day of July, anno Domini eighteen hundred and seventy-eight.

If conditions are broken, and continue so one year, the United States may complete the road.
SEC. 9. *And be it further enacted,* That the United States make the several conditional grants herein, and that the said Atlantic and Pacific Railroad Company accept the same, upon the further condition that if the said company make any breach of the conditions hereof, and allow the same to continue for upwards of one year, then, in such case, at any time hereafter, the United States may do any and all acts and things which may be needful and necessary to insure a speedy completion of the said road.

SEC. 10. *And be it further enacted,* That all people of the United Who may subscribe to stock. States shall have the right to subscribe to the stock of the Atlantic and Pacific Railroad Company until the whole capital named in this act of incorporation is taken up by complying with the terms of subscription.

SEC. 11. *And be it further enacted,* That said Atlantic and Pacific Railroad to be a post route and military road. railroad, or any part thereof, shall be a post route and military road, subject to the use of the United States for postal, military, naval and all other government service, and also subject Charges for Government transportation. to such regulations as Congress may impose restricting the charges for such government transportation.

Acceptance of these conditions by Company to be in writing, and within two years.
SEC. 12. *And be it further enacted,* That the acceptance of the terms, conditions and impositions of this act by the said Atlantic and Pacific Railroad Company shall be signified in writing under the corporate seal of said company, duly executed pursuant to the direction of its board of directors first had and obtained, which acceptance shall be made within two years after the passage of this act, and not afterwards, and shall be deposited in the office of the Secretary of the Interior.

SEC. 13. *And be it further enacted,* That the directors of said Annual report. company shall make and publish an annual report of their proceedings and expenditures, verified by the affidavits of the president and at least six of the directors, a copy of which shall be deposited in the office of said Secretary of the Interior, and they shall, from time to time, fix, determine and regulate the fares, tolls and charges to be received and paid for transportation of persons and property on said road or any part thereof.

SEC. 14. *And be it further enacted,* That the directors chosen in pursuance of the first section of this act shall, so soon as may be after their election, elect from their own number a president and vice-president; and said board of directors shall, from time to time, and so soon as may be after their election, choose a treasurer and secretary, who shall hold their offices at the will and pleasure of the board of directors. The treasurer and secretary shall give such bonds, with such security as the said board from time to time may require. The secretary shall, before entering upon his duty, be sworn to the faithful discharge thereof, and said oath shall be made a matter of record upon the books of said corporation. No person shall be a director of said company unless he shall be a stockholder, and qualified to vote for directors at the election at which he shall be chosen.

SEC. 15. *And be it further enacted,* That the president, vice-president and directors shall hold their offices for the period indicated in the by-laws of said company, not exceeding three years, respectively, and until others are chosen in their place and qualified. In case it shall so happen that an election of directors shall not be made on any day appointed by the by-laws of said company, the corporation shall not for that excuse be deemed to be dissolved, but such election may be holden on any day which shall be appointed by the directors. The directors, of whom seven, including the president, shall be a quorum for the transaction of business, shall have full power to make and prescribe such by-laws, rules and regulations as they shall deem needful and proper touching the disposition and management of the stock, property, estate and effects of the company, the transfer of shares, the duties and conduct of their officers and servants, touching the election and meeting of the directors, and all matters whatsoever which may appertain to the concerns of said company; and the said board of directors may have full power to fill any vacancy or vacancies that may occur from any cause or causes from time to time in their said board. And the said board of directors shall have power to appoint such engineers, agents and subordinates as may from time to time be necessary to carry into effect the object of the company, and to do all acts and things touching the location and construction of said road.

SEC. 16. *And be it further enacted,* That it shall be lawful for the directors of said company to require payment of the sum of ten per centum cash assessment upon all subscriptions received of all subscribers, and the balance thereof at such times and in such proportions and on such conditions as they shall deem to be necessary to complete the said road and telegraph lines within the time in this act prescribed. Sixty days previous notice shall be given of the payments required, and of the time and place of payment, by publishing a notice once a week in one daily newspaper in each of the cities of Boston, New York, Cincinnati, Saint Louis, Memphis and Nashville, and in case any stockholder shall neglect or refuse to pay, in pursuance of such notice, the stock held by such person shall be forfeited absolutely to the use of the company, and also any payment or payments that shall have been made on account thereof, subject to the condition that the board of directors may allow the redemption on such terms as they may prescribe.

SEC. 17. *And be it further enacted,* That the said company is authorized to accept to its own use any grant, donation, loan, power, franchise, aid, or assistance which may be granted to or conferred on said company by the Congress of the United States. by the Legislature of any State, or by any corporation, person or persons, or by any Indian tribe or nation through whose reservation the road herein provided for may pass; and said corporation is authorized to hold and enjoy any such grant, donation, loan, power, franchise, aid or assistance, to its own use, for the purpose aforesaid : *Provided,* That any such grant or donation, power, aid or assistance from any Indian tribe or nation shall be subject to the approval of the President of the United States.

SEC. 18. *And be it further enacted,* That the Southern Pacific Railroad, a company incorporated under the laws of the State of California, is hereby authorized to connect with the said Atlantic and Pacific Railroad, formed under this act, at such point, near the boundary line of the State of California, as they shall deem most suitable for a railroad line to San Francisco, and shall have a uniform gauge and rate of freight or fare with said road ; and in consideration thereof, to aid in its construction, shall have similar grants of land, subject to all the conditions and limitations herein provided, and shall be required to construct its road on the like

Marginal notes:

Ten per cent. of subscriptions to be paid in cash. Balance, when to be paid.

Notice when payments are due.

If stockholders neglect to pay, stock and previous payments forfeited.

Redemption.

Company may accept and hold any grant, loan, aid, &c.

Grant from any Indian tribe to be subject to the approval of the President of the United States.

Southern Pacific R. R. Co. may connect with the Atlantic and Pacific road.

Point of connection.

Gauge and rates of fare.

May have similar grants of land on like terms.

regulations, as to time and manner, with the Atlantic and Pacific Railroad herein provided for.

SEC. 19. *And be it further enacted*, That unless the said Atlantic and Pacific Railroad Company shall obtain bona fide subscriptions to the stock of said company to the amount of one million of dollars, with ten per centum paid, within two years after the passage of and approval of this act, it shall be null and void.

This Act to be void, unless, &c.

SEC. 20. *And be it further enacted*, That the better to accomplish the object of this act, namely, to promote the public interest and welfare by the construction of said railroad and telegraph line, and keeping the same in working order, and to secure to the government at all times, but particularly in time of war, the use and benefits of the same for postal, military and other purposes, Congress may, at any time, having due regard for the rights of said Atlantic and Pacific Railroad Company, add to, alter, amend or repeal this act.

Act may be altered or repealed.

SEC. 21. *And be it further enacted*, That whenever, in any grant of land or other subsidies, made, or hereafter to be made to railroads or other corporations, the United States has reserved the right, or shall reserve it, to appoint directors, engineers, commissioners or other agents to examine said roads, or act in conjunction with other officers of said company or companies, all the costs, charges and pay of said directors, engineers, commissioners or agents shall be paid by the respective companies. Said directors, engineers, commissioners or agents shall be paid for said services the sum of ten dollars per day, for each and every day actually and necessarily employed, and ten cents per mile for each and every mile actually and necessarily traveled, in discharging the duties required of them, which per diem and mileage shall be in full compensation for said services. And in case any company shall refuse or neglect to make such payments, no more patents for lands or other subsidies shall be issued to said company until these requirements are complied with.

When in grants to corporations, the United States reserves the right to appoint directors or agents, &c.; &c., of such persons are to be borne by the corporations.

Rate of pay to such persons.

If Company neglects to make such payments, no more patents for lands, &c., to issue.

APPROVED July 27th, 1866.

ACT EXTENDING TIME OF SOUTHERN PACIFIC RAILROAD COMPANY.

(Approved July 25, 1868.)

(15 U. S. Statutes at Large, page 187.)

Chap. CCXLII.

An Act to extend the Time for the Construction of the Southern Pacific Railroad in the State of California.

Time for Southern Pacific R. R. Co. of California to construct first section of road, &c., extended.

Rent of road, when to be built

Be it enacted by the Senate and House of Representatives of the United States of America in Congress assembled, That the Southern Pacific Railroad Company of the State of California shall, instead of the times now fixed by law for the construction of the first section of its road and telegraph line, have until the first day of July, eighteen hundred and seventy, for the construction of the first thirty miles, and they shall be required to construct at least twenty miles every year thereafter, and the whole line of their road within the time now provided by law.

APPROVED July 25, 1868.

[No. 87.]

JOINT RESOLUTION CONCERNING THE SOUTHERN PACIFIC RAILROAD OF CALIFORNIA.

(16 U. S. Statutes at Large, page 382.)

Southern Pacific Railroad Company may construct its road and telegraph line on the route, &c.

Be it resolved by the Senate and House of Representatives of the United States of America in Congress assembled, That the Southern Pacific Railroad Company of California may construct its road and telegraph line, as near as may be, on the route indicated by the map filed by said company in the Department of the Interior on the third day of January, eighteen hundred and sixty-seven ; and upon the construction of each section of said road, in the manner and within the time provided by law, and notice thereof being given by the company to the Secretary of the Interior, he shall direct an examination of each such section by commissioners to be appointed by the President, as provided in the act making a grant of land to said company, approved July twenty-seventh, eighteen hundred and sixty-six, and upon the report of the commissioners to the Secretary of the Interior that such section of said railroad and telegraph line has been constructed as required by law, it shall be the duty of the said Secretary of the Interior to cause patents to be issued to said company for the sections of land coterminous to each constructed section reported on as aforesaid, to the extent and amount granted to said company by the said act of July twenty-seventh, eighteen hundred and sixty-six, expressly saving and reserving all the rights of actual settlers, together with the other conditions and restrictions provided for in the third section of said act. *Patents for land to issue, when, &c., 1866, ch. 278, § 18, vol. xiv, p. 299.*

APPROVED, June 28, 1870.

SECTION 23D OF THE TEXAS PACIFIC RAILROAD ACT

(Approved March 3, 1871.)

(16 U. S. Statutes at Large, page 573–579.)

Chap. CXXII.

An Act to Incorporate the Texas Pacific Railroad Company, and to aid in the Construction of its Road, and for other purposes.

Be it enacted by the Senate and House of Representatives of the United States of America in Congress Assembled, &c. * * *

SEC. 23. That, for the purpose of connecting the Texas Pacific Railroad with the city of San Francisco, the Southern Pacific Railroad Company of California is hereby authorized (subject to the laws of California), to construct a line of railroad from a point at or near Tehachapa Pass, by way of Los Angeles, to the Texas Pacific Railroad, at or near the Colorado river, with the same rights, grants, and privileges, and subject to the same limitations, restric- *Southern Pacific Railroad Company may construct a road to connect the Texas Pacific with San Francisco.*

Proviso.

tions and conditions as were granted to said Southern Pacific Railroad Company of California by the act of July twenty-seven, eighteen hundred and sixty-six : *Provided, however,* That this section shall in no way affect or impair the rights, present or prospective, of the Atlantic and Pacific Railroad Company or any other railroad company.

APPROVED, March 3, 1871.

ACTS OF THE LEGISLATURE

OF THE

STATE OF CALIFORNIA

RELATIVE TO THE

SOUTHERN PACIFIC RAILROAD COMPANY.

———

CHAP. DXCI.

[STATUTES OF CALIFORNIA, 1865–6, PAGE 816.]

An Act to authorize all the Counties South of Santa Clara County to aid in the construction of the Southern Pacific Railroad.

(Approved April 2, 1866.)

The People of the State of California, represented in Senate and Assembly, do enact as follows :

SECTION 1.—It shall be lawful for the board of supervisors of any county into or through which the Southern Pacific Railroad Company, a corporation duly organized under the laws of this State, shall run their road, acting in behalf of the county, to donate aid to such railroad company in any sum not exceeding an amount equal to three per centum on the aggregate amount of the taxable property in such county, as

Authority to donate or subscribe.

9

shown by the last preceding assessment roll of the county ; or to subscribe to the capital stock of such railroad company in any sum not exceeding an amount equal to five per centum of the aggregate amount of the taxable property of the county, as shown by the last preceding assessment, as aforesaid : *Provided*, however, that the proposition so to donate or subscribe shall have been first submitted to and approved by the qualified electors of said county, and all the proceedings in relation thereto shall be conducted in accordance with the following provisions of this act, and not otherwise.

Proposition to b3 submitted to voters.

SEC. 2.—Whenever twenty-five or more of the taxpayers of any county into or through which the Southern Pacific Railroad Company shall run their road, representing twenty-five per cent. of the taxable property of such county, shall petition the board of supervisors, stating the fact that it is proposed· to run said railroad into or through said county, and asking the submission to the electors of the county, the proposition to donate aid to or subscribe for stock in said railroad company, in an amount to be named in said petition, which amount shall not exceed the limit fixed in the first section of this act, and stating specifically which proposition it is desired to have thus submitted, whether to donate or to subscribe, it shall be the duty of such board of supervisors, by proper order in that behalf, to grant such petition, and to submit the proposition so named to the electors of such county.

Petition to submit proposition.

SEC. 3.—For that purpose the board of supervisors shall order a special election to be holden throughout the county, the polls whereof shall be open in the several precincts or places for holding elections in such county on a day certain, to be named by them, which shall be not less than thirty nor more than sixty days from the date of such order or of the filing of such petition, at which election the proposition so named in such petition shall be submitted to the qualified electors of the county for their approval or rejection ; such board of supervisors shall cause notice of such election and of the proposition to be voted upon to be published in some newspaper printed in such county, if any be printed therein,

Special election,

Publication of notice.

and if not, then in some newspaper printed in an adjoining
county, for at least twenty days prior to such election, and a
like notice to be conspicuously posted at every place of opening the polls in said county, at least ten days prior to
said-election; the ballots cast at such election shall be in sub-
stantially the following form, viz.: If the proposition be to
make a donation, then such ballots shall have written or $_{\text{Ballots.}}$
printed thereon the words "donation of   dollars
(naming the amount) to the Southern Pacific Railroad Company;" if the proposition be to subscribe for stock, such ballots
shall have written or printed thereon the words "subscription
of   dollars (naming the amount) to the capital
stock of the Southern Pacific Railroad Company;" every ballot
given in favor of such proposition shall have the word "Yes"
written or printed thereon, and ever ballot against the same
shall have the word "No" written or printed thereon; such
elections shall be conducted in the same manner as elections $_{\text{Returns.}}$
for county officers, and in like manner the votes cast thereat
shall be counted and sealed returns thereof made; and on the
second Monday after such election, or at such other time as
the board of supervisors may have fixed therefor, said returns
shall be opened and canvassed, and the result declared in the
same manner as in case of election for county officers.

SEC. 4.—If upon such canvass it shall be found that a $_{\text{Approval or}}$
greater number of the electors of the county, voting upon the $_{\text{rejection.}}$
proposition so submitted, have voted "No," than have voted
"Yes," then such proposition shall be deemed and declared to
have been rejected, and the fact of such rejection shall be duly
entered upon the record of the proceedings of the board of
supervisors, and no further action shall be had in relation
thereto. But if upon such canvass it shall be found that a
greater number of the electors of said county, voting upon the
proposition so submitted, have voted "Yes" than have voted
"No," then such proposition shall be deemed and declared to
have been approved, a record of the fact of such approval shall
be made upon the minutes of the board of supervisors, and
said board, by their clerk, shall, in writing, notify such railroad
company of the proposition which has been so submitted, and
of the approval thereof.

Sec. 5.—Before any further action in the premises shall be taken by such board of supervisors, said railroad company shall file in the office of the clerk of said board, a notice under the seal of the corporation, stating whether said company accepts the subscription or donation so tendered by said county, and if accepted, there shall also be filed therewith a copy of the certificate of incorporation or articles of association of said company, certified by the secretary of state, and such copy shall thereafter be kept on file in such office, for the information of such board of supervisors and of the citizens of said county.

Acceptance to be filed.

Sec. 6.—If such proposed donation or subscription is accepted, then immediately upon the filing of such notice and of a certified copy of the articles of association, as mentioned in the last section, or as soon thereafter as practicable, it shall be the duty of the board of supervisors of such county, and they are hereby authorized and directed, if the proposition so approved shall be one in favor of subscription to the capital stock of said company, to make such subscription, on the subscription books of said company, through a committee consisting of two members of such board of supervisors, who shall be, by an order of the board, entered upon their minutes, duly authorized for that purpose, and to pledge therefor and for the due payment of such subscription, in accordance with the provisions of this act, the good faith of the county; or if the proposition so approved be one in favor of a donation to said company, then such board of supervisors shall pass an order, and enter the same on their journal, declaring the good faith of the county pledged to make such donation in the bonds of the county, in such amounts and under such conditions as are named in this act.

Making subscription or donation.

Sec. 7.—If, in compliance with a vote so had as aforesaid, subscription be made by any county to the capital stock of said railroad company, the same shall be made and accepted with the condition that such subscription shall be payable in the bonds of the county, to be issued as hereinafter directed, and not otherwise, and for such subscription such bonds shall be received at par, dollar for dollar.

To be made in bonds of county.

Sec. 8.—In all cases of donation in aid of, or of subscription **How paid.** to, the capital stock of said railroad company by any county under the provisions of this act, the same shall be paid in instalments of not less than ten nor more than twenty per cent. as the work on such road shall progress, and in no case shall an instalment of the bonds of any county be issued to said railroad company until an amount, at least equal thereto has been expended by said company in the actual graduation of **How to be expended.** such railroad or other work necessary to its construction or completion, nor shall a second instalment be paid to such company until the first has been expended on the road, or in purchase of iron or rolling stock or other material therefor.

Sec. 9.—In all cases where a county has made a donation in aid of, or has subscribed to, the capital stock of said railroad company, under the provisions of this act, it shall be the duty of the secretary and engineer in charge of such railroad company, **Report to be made to Supervisors.** from time to time, as the bonds of such county are required to be issued, to make report in writing, under oath, and lay the same before the board of supervisors of such county, showing the progress of the work on the railroad, and the amount and cost thereof, together with the cost of bridging, ties, and other material for the superstructure, and of the iron and rolling stock which may have been purchased or contracted for said railroad ; and if after the issuance of the first or any subsequent instalment of bonds to said railroad company, under the provisions of this act, there should be any failure or refusal on the part of said company to expend such bonds in the mode and manner herein provided in the construction of said railroad, or purchase of materials therefor, then and in that event the board of supervisors of such county may, at their option, withhold any further payment of instalments of the amount donated **Withholding instalments.** or subscribed to said railroad, as the case may be, and they shall not be liable to any further calls thereon, and if so declared by the board of supervisors, such donation or subscription shall be held void and of no effect, and said company shall be liable to such county for such amounts as may have been paid on such donation or subscription, which shall be recoverable at law, in any court of competent jurisdiction.

SEC. 10.—The board of supervisors of any county do-
nating aid to, or subscribing to the capital stock of the said railroad company, under the provisions of this act, shall, from time to time, as such donation or subscription shall become due and be demanded by the board of directors of said company, cause bonds of the county to be issued and delivered to said railroad company for such an amount as may be due, but not exceeding, at any one time, twenty per cent. of such donation or subscription, as hereinbefore provided; and the officers hereinafter mentioned shall, each and every of them, execute and countersign said bonds, as herein provided, whenever so directed by an order of the board of supervisors of such county; such bonds shall be issued in sums of one thousand dollars each, shall be numbered consecutively from number one onward through all the bonds issued to said company, shall be made payable to said railroad company, giving its corporate name, or to the holder or bearer thereof, on a specified day, to be named in said bonds, which shall be twenty years after the date of the issuance thereof, at the office of the treasurer of such county, and shall bear interest at the rate of eight per cent. per annum from the date of their issue; the interest upon such bonds shall be due and payable semi-annually so long as such bonds are outstanding and unpaid, and shall be payable at the office of such treasurer, on a specified day, to be named in the interest-coupons which shall be attached to such bonds, as hereinafter provided; both principal and interest of such bonds shall be made payable in United States gold coin, dollar for dollar; such bonds shall be signed by the chairman of the board of supervisors, by the auditor and the clerk of such county, as such officers, the auditor making and keeping in his office an accurate account of all bonds so signed, with the number, date and amount of each, and the clerk shall cause the seal of the county to be affixed to each of said bonds, and the chairman of such board shall forthwith deliver the same to the company entitled thereto, taking the receipt of the secre- tary of said company therefor, which receipt shall be executed in triplicate, and shall set forth the number, date and amount of each bond so delivered; such chairman shall thereupon file one of such receipts in the office of the clerk of said county, one in the office of the auditor, and one in the office of the treas-

urer of such county, and shall make report to the board of supervisors of the proceedings in the premises at the next meeting thereof.

SEC. 11. All bonds issued under the provisions of this act shall Coupons. have coupons for the interest attached, so that the same may be removed without mutilation of the bonds ; such coupons shall each be for one half year's interest upon the bond to which it is attached ; they shall be numbered from one to forty, consecutively; each shall specify the number of the bond to which it is attached, the amount to become due upon such coupon, and the day when it is payable, and each shall be signed by the auditor of the county for which it is issued. When any interest shall be paid upon any bond issued under the provisions of this act, the county treasurer paying the same shall receive the coupon for the interest so paid, shall cancel the Cancellation. same by writing across the face thereof the word "Paid," with the date of payment and his official signature, and shall thereupon deliver the same to the auditor of said county, taking his receipt in duplicate therefor, one copy of which said treasurer shall file in his own office, and the other copy of which he shall deliver to the clerk of said county, and thereupon such clerk shall report the same to the board of supervisors of such county at the next meeting thereof.

SEC. 12.—When any county shall have donated aid to or subscribed to the capital stock of said railroad company as herein provided, it shall be the duty of the board of super- Levy of tax. visors of such county, at the same time of levying other taxes in said county (or in the first year at any time before the making out of the duplicate of the general assessment list for such county), in each year to levy a tax sufficient to raise the amount of interest falling due within each year, and not less than two nor more than five per cent. of the principal of such bonds, which shall be paid into a fund to be styled the Railroad Fund ; the taxes provided in this section shall be levied and collected at the same time, and in the same manner as taxes for county purposes, and when collected shall be paid into the county treasury, and shall be kept separate from How applied. other funds of the county, and be applied as follows: .

First.—To the payment of the interest as it falls due.

Second.—To the payment and redemption of such bonds as hereinafter provided.

Sec. 13.—Whenever there shall be in the Railroad Fund of any county after providing for the interest of the current year, a sum of money amounting to three thousand dollars or upwards, it shall be the duty of the county treasurer to advertise in a newspaper published in such county, if any newspaper be published therein, and if not, then in a newspaper published in the next adjoining county, and also in at least one newspaper published in the city and county of San Francisco, once in each week for four weeks, for sealed proposals for the redemption of bonds, stating the amount of money on hand applicable to that purpose, and ten days from the expiration of the time for such publication, said treasurer shall open the proposals so received, and such bonds as shall be surrendered by the holders thereof, at the lowest proposed rate, and having all the unpaid coupons thereto attached, shall be paid off and liquidated so far as the fund on hand will go for that purpose, *provided*, however, that such proposed rate shall not be for more than the par value of such bond, and the interest already accrued and unpaid thereon ; *and provided* further that should there be no proposals made for less than par value as aforesaid, then the fund on hand shall be applied in payment of such bonds, and the interest then actually accrued and unpaid, in the order of the number of their issue, the county treasurer giving four weeks' notice, in the manner hereinbefore provided, of the numbers of said bond to which the fund on hand will be applied, and requesting their presentation for payment, after which time such bonds, if not presented, shall cease to draw interest. When all the bonds so issued shall have been liquidated, redeemed and paid off, any moneys remaining on hand in the railroad fund shall be paid into the general fund of the county. In all cases of the liquidation or payment of bonds issued under the provision of this act, the same course shall be pursued, in reference to canceling, filing, receipting for and reporting the same, as is hereinbefore provided upon the payment of interest coupons.

Redemption of bonds.

Transfer of fund.

Cancellation of bonds.

SEC. 14.—Whenever any county shall have subscribed to the capital stock of said railroad company under the provisions of this act, such county shall possess all the rights and powers of any stockholder in such company, and the board of supervisors may from time to time, as occasion shall require, appoint one of their own number or any citizen of said county to represent said county at any meeting of the stockholders of said company, and to cast any and all votes at such meeting which said county, if a natural person holding the same amount of stock, would be entitled to cast, and generally, on behalf of such county to do any and all things pertaining to the business of said company which a natural person holding stock therein might or could lawfully do. A certified copy of the order of the board of supervisors, under the seal of the county, filed with the secretary of said company, shall be the evidence of the authority of the person therein named to act on behalf of such county. Casting votes to which stock belonging to county is entitled.

SEC. 15.—Whenever any county shall make a donation in aid of said railroad company under the provisions of this act, the same shall be made and accepted (if the same is accepted) upon the express condition that said railroad company shall at any and all times after the opening of its railroad to general business, if so required, transport all prisoners being taken to the jail of such county, or from the jail to the place of trial, and the officers having them in charge, and any and all materials for the construction or repair of the court house or jail of such county over said railroad free of charge. Prisoners and officers in charge to travel to and from jail free.

SEC. 16.—All officers having any duty to perform under the provisions of this act shall be allowed the same rate of compensation therefor as is allowed for other similar service, to be fixed by the board of supervisors and paid out of the general fund of the county. Compensation.

SEC. 17.—All taxes, except State taxes, paid by said railroad company receiving county bonds under this act in the county issuing such bonds, instead of being distributed into the several funds of the county like other taxes, and all dividends Railroad taxes to be part of railroad fund.

10

paid by said company to said county shall be paid into and form a part of the railroad fund so long as any such bond shall remain outstanding and unpaid; *provided* this act shall not apply to the counties of Alameda, Santa Clara or San Francisco.

\

Chapter DXLII.

[Statutes of California, 1867–8, page 716.]

An Act to confer power upon the Board of Supervisors of the city and county of San Francisco.

(Approved March 30, 1868.)

The People of the State of California, represented in Senate and Assembly, do enact as follows:

Authorized to sell railroad stocks.

SECTION 1. The Board of Supervisors of the city and county of San Francisco is hereby authorized and empowered to dispose of, to the Southern Pacific Railroad Company, the shares of stock of the San Francisco & San José Railroad Company, owned or held by the said city and county, upon such terms and subject to such conditions as the said Board may think expedient.

Proviso.

The proceeds of all sales shall be paid into the treasury of the said city and county, *provided* that no disposition of said shares of stock to the Southern Pacific Railroad Company shall be effectual to vest the title to said shares in said company until it shall have completed and put in operation its section of railroad from San José to Gilroy.

SEC. 2. This act shall take effect immediately.

GRANT OF LAND IN SAN FRANCISCO TO THE SOUTHERN PACIFIC RAILROAD COMPANY FOR A TERMINUS.

Chapter DXLIII.

[Statutes of California, 1867–8, page 716.]

An Act to survey and dispose of certain salt marsh and tide lands belonging to the State of California.

(Approved March 30, 1868.)

The People of the State of California, represented in Senate and Assembly, do enact as follows:

SECTION 1. The Governor of the State shall appoint three persons, who shall constitute a Board of Tide-Land Commissioners, and shall hold office for two years from the date of their appointment, and shall have the charge and disposition of all the salt marsh and tide lands belonging to the State of California situated in the city and county of San Francisco, as hereinafter provided by this act, and who shall be known and designated in this act as "the Commissioners." *Commissioners to be appointed.*

SEC. 2. (Official bonds, oaths and penalties.)

SEC. 3. (President and secretary, and their duties.)

SEC. 4. The commissioners shall take possession of all the salt marsh and tide lands, and lands lying under water, to the point that may be established as the water-front, situate along *Duties of Commissioners.*

the Bay of San Francisco, and situate in the city and county of San Francisco, belonging to the State of California, and have the same surveyed to a point not beyond twenty-four feet

water at the lowest stage of the tide, and cause to be prepared two maps of the same, showing the quantity and extent of the property situated as aforesaid, and exhibiting all the municipal subdivisions, streets, alleys, blocks, squares and lots, which lots shall not exceed in area six thousand two hundred and sixty-one and one-sixth square feet each. One of said maps they shall retain in their office at San Francisco, and the other they shall file in the office of the State surveyor.

After such preliminary survey the commissioners, in conjunction. with the governor of the State, the mayor of San Francisco, and the president of the Chamber of Commerce of San Francisco, and who shall be known and designated in this act as the "State Board," shall meet, and by a two-thirds vote, establish the water-line front of San Francisco ; but they shall not have power to alter, in any manner whatever, the water-line front of said city north of the terminus of Second street, as established by the act passed March twenty-sixth, eighteen hundred and fifty-one.

After the establishment of the water-line front as above provided, the commissioners shall have all the property lying within the same belonging to the State surveyed, subject to the approval of the State board, into lots and blocks in accordance with the official map survey of the city of San Francisco, reserving so much thereof for streets, docks, piers, slips, canals, drains, or other use necessary for the public convenience and the purposes of commerce, as in their judgment may be required, and have two maps of the same prepared showing the property as re-surveyed to the water-line front, the streets, blocks, reservations, and everything necessary to be shown by such maps, one of which maps shall be filed in the surveyor-general's office, and the other shall remain in their office at San Francisco ; *provided* that the land belonging or granted to the California Dry Dock Company, and the overflowed land in

front thereof, shall be, and the same is hereby, excepted from the operation of this act ; *provided that there is hereby granted and donated to the Southern Pacific Railroad Company and the*

Western Pacific Railroad Company, for a terminus in the city and county of San Francisco, to each of said companies, thirty acres, exclusive of streets, basins, public squares and docks, out of the aforesaid land, and lying southwardly from Channel street, and outside of the line known as the red line water-front of Mission Bay, to be located jointly or severally by the said respective companies within ninety days from the passage of this act, in a manner and form to be approved by the governor, the mayor of the city and county of San Francisco, and the president of the Chamber of Commerce of said city, or a majority of them, and so as not to extend beyond twenty-four feet of water at low tide, nor within three hundred feet of such line as may be established, under the provisions of this act, as the permanent water-line front of said city, together with the use of a right of way for said companies to said terminus over the lands of this State for the road-beds and tracks of said company—the board of commissioners herein named to fix and designate the lands (not to exceed a strip two hundred feet in width for both said companies) over which said right of way shall be exercised; and *provided* that such grant of land for terminus and the said right of way shall not be construed to interfere with the proper establishment and regulation of streets and alleys, docks, wharves and basins, culverts and sewers, and the laying down of gas and water pipes by the proper authorities of the city and county of San Francisco, and the authorities of said city and county of San Francisco shall have such jurisdiction and control over said streets and crossings thereof as is or may be conferred by law in other cases; and said railroad companies shall so construct their roads as to cause the least obstruction to travel over and along their roads, and at the crossings thereof; *provided* that in case either of the said companies shall fail to comply with the conditions of this act, such company shall forfeit their rights thereunder; and in such event the other company accepting and using the same for the purposes indicated shall receive thirty acres (exclusive of streets, basins, public squares and docks) for terminal purposes, and not exceeding one hundred feet in width for right of way; and the said companies are hereby authorized to extend their roads or purchase other roads so as to reach their terminus. And upon the location

Rights reserved to city and county.

Forfeiture.

by the said companies of their terminus and terminal depots
Conditions of
donation. and stations upon the said premises, and the expenditure of
one hundred thousand dollars thereon by each of said com-
panies, the governor shall issue patents therefor to the said
companies respectively ; *provided* that unless the said companies shall, within thirty months from the passage of this act,
make the terminus of their roads upon the said premises, and
expend thereon the said sum of one hundred thousand dollars
each, then any grant herein contained shall be void as to the
said company so in default, and the lands herein granted to
such company shall revert to and be the property of the
State ; *provided* that nothing in this act shall be construed
to interfere with the collection of dockage and wharfage by
Rights reserv-
ed to State the State, nor with the right of the State to construct, adjoining the property granted, such wharves and docks as may, from
time to time, be provided by law ; *provided, further,* that if the
two hundred feet herein mentioned for the right of way, or any
part thereof, shall at any time be abandoned or cease to be
used as such roadway by said companies, then so much thereof
as shall be so abandoned or disused shall revert to the State ;
and *provided,* further, that if the said railroad companies, or
either of them, shall not, within thirty days of the organization of the board of commissioners, notify such board of the
acceptance of the provisions of this donation and grant, the
lands herein proposed to be donated and granted to the said
company or companies so failing to notify said board shall be
sold at auction, as is otherwise provided in this act ; and in
the event said companies, or either of them, shall accept the
grant or donation herein made, the same shall be in lieu of all
other grants of land made or to be made to the company accepting the same in the city and county of San Francisco, at
the present session of the Legislature ; *provided* that no part
of said land granted or donated to said railroad companies
shall be located on any land now in the *bona fide* possession
and occupation of any citizen or citizens of this State.

SEC. 5, &c. (Sale of State lands within water-line—how
made, &c., &c.)

Chapter CXVI.

[Statutes of California, 1869-70, page 107.]

An Act relating to Certificates of Incorporation.

(Approved March 1, 1870.)

The People of the State of California, represented in Senate and Assembly, do enact as follows :

SECTION 1. Any corporation, now or hereafter organized under the laws of this State, may amend its articles of association or certificate of incorporation by a majority vote of the board of directors or trustees, and by a vote or written assent of the stockholders representing at least two-thirds of the capital stock of such corporation, and a copy of the said articles of association or certificate of incorporation, as thus amended, duly certified to be correct, by the president and secretary of the board of directors or trustees of such corporation, shall be filed in the same office or offices where the original articles or certificate are required by law to be filed, and from the time of filing such copy of the amended articles or certificate, such corporation shall have the same powers, and it and the stockholders thereof shall be thereafter subject to the same liabilities as if such amendment had been embraced in the original articles or certificate ; *provided* that the time of the existence of such corporation shall not be thereby extended beyond the time fixed in the original articles or certificate ; and *provided*, further, that such original and amended articles or certificate shall, together, contain all the matters and things required by the law under which the original articles of association or certificate of incorporation were executed and filed ; and *provided*, further, that nothing herein contained shall be construed to cure or amend any defect existing in any original certificate of incorporation heretofore filed, by reason of the failure of such certificate to set forth the matters required by law to make the same valid as a certificate of incorporation at the time of the filing thereof ; also *provided* that unless the vote or written assent of all the stockholders has been obtained,

Amended certificates of incorporation.

then a notice of the intention to make such amendment shall first be advertised for sixty days in some newspaper published in the town or county in which the principal place of business of said company is located; and the written protest of any one of said stockholders, or his duly authorized agent or attorney, whose assent has not been obtained, filed with the secretary of the said company, shall, unless withdrawn, be effectual to prevent the adoption of such amendment, *provided* that nothing in this act shall be construed to authorize any corporation to diminish its capital stock.

SEC. 2. This act shall take effect and be in force from and after its passage.

Chapter CCCCLXI.

[Statutes of California, 1869-70, p. 669.]

An Act to extend the time allowed to the Southern Pacific Railroad Company and the Western Pacific Railroad Company in which to make the terminus of their roads upon certain lands donated to them by the State for that purpose in the City and County of San Francisco.

(Approved April 2, 1870.)

The People of the State of California, represented in Senate and Assembly, do enact as follows:

Time extended. SECTION 1. The time within which the Southern Pacific Railroad Company and the Western Pacific Railroad Company are required to make the terminus of their roads, and expend thereon the sum of one hundred thousand dollars each, upon certain salt marsh and tide lands in the city and county of San Francisco, donated to said companies for that purpose, by an act entitled " An Act to survey and dispose of certain salt marsh and tide lands belonging to the State of California," approved March thirtieth, one thousand eight hundred and sixty-eight, is hereby extended eighteen months, and the location of said lands for terminal purposes, made under the provisions of said act, is hereby approved.

SEC. 2. This act shall take effect from and after its passage.

Chapter CCCCLXXXIV.

[Statutes of California, 1869–70, page 707.]

An Act to empower the City and County of San Francisco to aid in the construction of the Southern Pacific Railroad, and other purposes.

(Approved April 2, 1870.)

The People of the State of California, represented in Senate and Assembly, do enact as follows :

SECTION 1. It shall be the duty of the board of supervisors of the city and county of San Francisco to order a special election Special election. to be held in said city and county of San Francisco on the first Tuesday in June next, for the purpose of submitting to the qualified electors of said city and county of San Francisco, the proposition for the said city and county of San Francisco to issue and deliver to the Southern Pacific Railroad Company, its successors or assigns, county bonds in aid of and for and in consideration of the construction of a railroad by said company, its successors or assigns, from the town of Gilroy, in a southerly direction.

SEC. 2. It shall be the duty of the board of supervisors of said city and county to cause notice of at least twenty days to Notice. be given by publication in one or more daily newspapers published in the said city and county, and by posting written or

11

printed notices thereof at each place of holding said election in said city and county, stating in such publications and notices the proposition to be submitted to the electors of said city and county, and the time and manner of voting thereon.

Ballots.

Every ballot cast in said city and county in favor of said proposition shall have the words " For the issuing of bonds for the Southern Pacific Railroad" printed or written thereon ; and every ballot cast in opposition to said proposition shall have the words "Against the issuing of bonds for the Southern Pacific Railroad" printed or written thereon. Said election shall be conducted under the provisions of an act entitled "An Act to regulate elections", passed March twenty-third, eighteen

Election, how conducted.

hundred and fifty, and the several acts amendatory thereof and supplemental thereto, and an act to provide for the registration of the citizens of this State, and for the enrollment in the several election districts of all the legal voters thereof, and for the prevention and punishment of frauds affecting the elective franchise, approved March nineteenth, eighteen hundred and sixty-six, and the several acts amendatory thereof and supplemental thereto, so far as applicable.

Result.

SEC. 3. If at said election a greater number of the electors of said city and county, voting upon said proposition, shall vote for the issuing of bonds for the Southern Pacific Railroad than shall vote against the issuing of bonds for the Southern Pacific Railroad, then the board of supervisors of said city and county so voting in favor of such proposition shall, under the conditions and in the amounts, and as is hereinafter prescribed, issue to the Southern Pacific Railroad Company, its successors or assigns, city and county bonds, bearing seven per cent. interest, payable semi-annually, both principal and interest payable in United States gold coin.

Issue of bonds.

SEC. 4. Upon satisfactory proof being made, by affidavits or otherwise, to the board of supervisors of the city and county of San Francisco, that the track of said Southern Pacific Railroad has been laid, and that engines and cars are running thereon from the town of Gilroy to a point fifty miles therefrom, in a southerly direction on the line of said road as hereafter constructed, then the board of supervisors of said city and county of San Francisco shall issue, as hereinafter provided, to said railroad company, its successors or assigns, the city and county bonds of said city and county of San Francisco, to the extent of two hundred and fifty bonds of one thousand dollars each ; and upon the filing of like proof with the clerk of the aforesaid board of supervisors, that the track of said road has been laid, and that engines and cars are running thereon for one hundred consecutive miles from the town of Gilroy, then the aforesaid board of supervisors of said city and county of San Francisco shall issue as hereinafter provided, to said railroad company, its successors or assigns, additional bonds of said city and county, to the extent of two hundred and fifty bonds of one thousand dollars each ; and upon the filing of like proof with the clerk of the aforesaid board of supervisors, that the track of said road has been laid, and that engines and cars are running thereon for fifty additional miles on said road, making one hundred and fifty miles from the town of Gilroy, then the board of supervisors of said city and county of San Francisco shall issue, as hereinafter provided, to said railroad company, its successors and assigns, additional city and county bonds, to the extent of two hundred and fifty bonds of one thousand dollars each ; and upon the filing of like proof with the aforesaid clerk that the track of the aforesaid Southern Pacific Railroad Company has been laid, and that engines and cars are running thereon for fifty additional miles on said road, being two hundred consecutive miles from the town of Gilroy, then the said board of supervisors of the said city and county of San Francisco shall issue to said company, its successors or assigns, as hereinafter provided, additional city and county bonds, to the extent of two hundred and fifty bonds of one thousand dollars each.

SEC. 5. Upon proof being made, by affidavit or otherwise, as provided in the foregoing sections, to the supervisors of the said city and county therein named, the mayor and the treasurer of the said city and county shall draw and issue bonds forthwith, and in denominations of one thousand dollars each, in such total amounts as hereinbefore prescribed for said city and county. Said bonds shall draw interest at the rate of seven per cent.

Interest. per annum from the date of issue, payable upon the first day of January and the first day of July of each year, at the office of the treasurer of the city and county, until said bonds are redeemed. The principal of said bonds shall be made payable in twenty years from the date of issue.

Bonds, by whom signed. Said bonds of the city and county of San Francisco shall be signed by the mayor and treasurer of said city and county as such officers, and when signed shall be countersigned by the clerk of the said city and county of San Francisco, and the board of supervisors shall cause the fact of the signing and countersigning of said bonds to be entered upon their journal, together with the number, date and amount of each bond so signed and countersigned ; and upon the countersigning of said bonds, the seal of the said city and county shall be affixed to each bond by the clerk thereof ; and said clerk shall

Delivery. then deliver the said bonds thus signed, countersigned and sealed, to the authorized agent of such railroad company, its successors or assigns ; which delivery shall take place immediately after the signing, countersigning and sealing thereof, as herein provided ; and said clerk so delivering said bonds shall take a receipt in duplicate for said bonds so issued and delivered from the secretary of such company, setting forth in said receipts the numbers dates and amounts of said bonds.

Coupons. SEC. 6. Forty coupons for the interest shall be attached to each bond, so that the coupons can be removed without mutilation to the bond. Said coupons shall be signed by the treasurer of said city and county.

Condition of delivery. SEC. 7. The issue and the delivery of the bonds of the city and county of San Francisco to said Southern Pacific Railroad Company shall be on the express condition that said Southern Pacific Railroad Company, its successors and assigns, shall establish, continue and maintain its terminus and passenger and freight depots in said city and county until the principal and interest of said bonds are due and fully paid ; and to enable said company, its successors or assigns, to reach its said

depots and its lands in Mission Bay, donated by the State of
California, by such route as may be approved by the mayor or
county judge of the city and county of San Francisco, the said
railroad company, its successors or assigns, is authorized to
make such arrangements with the San Francisco & San José
Railroad Company as may be necessary to accomplish said
objects ; and for that purpose said last-named company is empowered to do all necessary acts and things, and also to extend
its road to said depots and lands by such route as may be approved by the mayor or county judge of the city and county
of San Francisco as aforesaid.

SEC. 8. This act shall take effect, and be in force, from and
after its passage.

Chapter DLXXIX.

[Statutes of California, 1869–70, page 883.]

*An Act to aid in giving effect to an Act of Congress relating to the
Southern Pacific Railroad Company.*

(Approved April 4, 1870.)

*The People of the State of California, represented in Senate and
Assembly, do enact as follows :*

SECTION I. Whereas, by the provisions of a certain act of
Congress of the United States of America, entitled "An Act
granting lands to aid in the construction of a railroad and telegraph line from San Francisco to the eastern line of the State
of California," approved July twenty-seventh, eighteen hundred
and sixty-six, certain grants were made to, and certain rights,
privileges, powers and authority were vested in and conferred
upon the Southern Pacific Railroad Company, a corporation
duly organized and existing under the laws of the State of
California : therefore, to enable the said company to more fully
and completely comply with and perform the requirements, provisions and conditions of the said act of Congress, and all
other acts of Congress now in force, or which may hereafter

May change line
of railroad.

be enacted, the State of California hereby consents to said act, and the said company, its successors and assigns, are hereby authorized and empowered to change the line of its railroad so as to reach the eastern boundary line of the State of California by such route as the company shall determine to be the most practicable, and to file new and amendatory articles of association, and the right, power and privilege is hereby granted to, conferred upon and vested in them to construct, maintain and operate by steam, or other power, the said railroad and telegraph line mentioned in said acts of Congress, hereby confirming to and vesting in the said company, its successors and assigns, all the rights, privileges, franchises, power and authority conferred upon, granted to or vested in said company by the said acts of Congress, and any act of Congress which may be hereafter enacted.

SEC. II. This act shall take effect, and be in force, from and after its passage.

Chapter CCXVII.

[Statutes of California 1871-2, Page 282.]

An Act to extend the time allowed to the Southern Pacific Railroad Company and the Western Pacific Railroad Company in which to make the terminus of their roads upon certain lands donated to them by the State for that purpose in the City and County of San Francisco.

(Approved March 6, 1872.)

The People of the State of California, represented in Senate and Assembly, do enact as follows:

Extension of time.

SECTION 1. The time within which the Southern Pacific Railroad Company and the Western Pacific Railroad Company are required to make the terminus of their roads and expend thereon the sum of one hundred thousand dollars each upon certain salt marsh and tide lands in the city and county of San Francisco, donated to said companies for that purpose by an act entitled "An act to survey and dispose of certain salt marsh and tide lands belonging to the State of California," approved March thirtieth, one thousand eight hundred and sixty-eight, as extended by an act entitled "An Act to extend the time allowed to the Southern Pacific Railroad Company and the Western Pacific Railroad Company, in which to make the terminus of their roads upon certain lands donated to them by the State for that purpose in the city and county of San Francisco," approved April second, one thousand eight hundred and seventy, is hereby extended three months.

SEC. 2 This act shall take effect from and after its passage.

SUPPLEMENT.

CONTINUATION OF ARTICLES OF ASSOCIATION OF THE SOUTHERN
PACIFIC R. R. Co.—From page 43.

VIII.

ARTICLES OF ASSOCIATION

OF THE

SOUTHERN PACIFIC BRANCH RAILROAD CO.

(Endorsed)—Filed in the office of the Secretary of State,
December 23d, 1872.

DRURY MELONE,
Secretary of State.
By H. H. RUSSELL,
Deputy.

Recorded Book 2, }
Folio 408.   }

STATE OF CALIFORNIA, }
Department of State. }

I, Drury Melone, Secretary of State of the State of California, do hereby certify that I have compared the annexed copy of Articles of Association of the Southern Pacific Branch Railroad Company with the original now on file in my office, and that the same is a correct transcript therefrom and of the whole thereof.

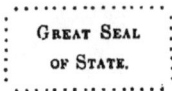

GREAT SEAL
OF STATE.

Witness my hand and the great seal of State, at office in Sacramento, California, the 15th day of August, A. D. 1873.

DRURY MELONE,
Secretary of State.
By H. H. RUSSELL,
Deputy.

ARTICLES OF ASSOCIATION

OF THE

SOUTHERN PACIFIC BRANCH RAILROAD COMPANY.

Know all men by these presents, that we, the undersigned, being subscribers to the capital stock of a contemplated railroad from a point on the Southern Pacific Railroad at or near Salinas City, in Monterey County, southeasterly to a point in Kern County, south of Tulare Lake, intersecting the San Joaquin Valley Division of the said Southern Pacific Railroad; also from a point on the above described line at or near San Miguel, in San Luis Obispo County, thence in a southerly direction to a point of intersection in Los Angeles County with the line of the Southern Pacific Railroad running from Tahechepah Pass by way of Los Angeles to Fort Yuma; which stock so subscribed by us amounts to not less than one thousand dollars per mile for each mile of said railroad, and ten per cent. in cash has been actually and in good faith paid thereon to E. H. Miller, Jr., one of the number who has been by us appointed temporary treasurer, and being desirous of forming a corporation do hereby, at a regular meeting of said stockholders, held pursuant to due notice thereof in writing, given by said treasurer, adopt the following:

ARTICLES OF ASSOCIATION.

ARTICLE FIRST.—We, the undersigned, do hereby form and organize ourselves into a corporation, under and in pursuance of an act of the State of California, entitled "An Act to provide for the incorporation of railroad companies and the management of the affairs thereof and other matters relating thereto," approved May 20th, 1861, and of the several acts supplementary thereto and amendatory thereof, for the purpose of purchasing, constructing, owning, maintaining and operating a railroad from a point on the Southern Pacific Railroad at or near

Salinas City, in the county of Monterey, southeasterly to a point in Kern County south of Tulare Lake, intersecting the San Joaquin Valley Division of the said Southern Pacific Railroad; also from a point on the above described line at or near San Miguel, in San Luis Obispo County, thence in a southerly direction to a point of intersection in Los Angeles County, with the line of the Southern Pacific Railroad running from Taheechepah Pass by way of Los Angeles to Fort Yuma. The counties into or through which the said railroad is intended to pass are Monterey, San Luis Obispo, Kern, Santa Barbara and Los Angeles.

ARTICLE SECOND.—The name of the said corporation is and shall be the "Southern Pacific Branch Railroad Company." The time of the existence of the said company shall be fifty years. And the length of the proposed railroad, as near as may be, is one hundred and eighty miles for the first described part, and two hundred and forty miles for the second described part, being an aggregate of four hundred and twenty miles.

ARTICLE THIRD.—The capital stock of the said corporation shall be twenty millions dollars, being the actual contemplated cost of constructing said railroad, together with the cost of the right of way, motive power and every other appurtenance and thing, for the completion and running of said road, as nearly as can be estimated by competent engineers.

Said capital stock shall consist of and be divided into two hundred thousand shares of one hundred dollars each.

ARTICLE FOURTH.—The number of directors to manage the affairs of said corporation shall be five, and the names of the persons chosen to act as such directors, and to hold their offices, until others are duly elected, are, E. H. Miller, Jr., Albert Gallatin, B. B. Redding, Benjamin R. Crocker and Charles H. Cummings, all of whom are subscribers to these articles of association.

In testimony whereof, we have hereunto severally subscribed our names, places of residence and the number of said shares of stock held by each, this 20th day of December, 1872.

NAMES.	RESIDENCE.	No. OF SHARES.	AMOUNT.
E. H. Miller, Jr.	Sacramento.	Five.	$500
Albert Gallatin	"	Five.	500
W. R. S. Foye	"	Five.	500
C. H. Cummings	"	Five.	500
E. J. Robinson	"	Five.	500
Leland Stanford	"	2,085 shares.	208,500
Mark Hopkins	"	2,085 "	208,500
Benjamin B. Redding	"	Five.	500
E. W. Hopkins	"	Five.	500
B. R. Crocker	"	Five.	500
		4,210 shares.	$421,000

STATE OF CALIFORNIA, } ss. :
County of Sacramento, }

On this twenty-third day of December, A. D. 1872, personally appeared before the undersigned, a notary public in and for said county of Sacramento, Charles H. Cummings, E. H. Miller, Jr., and Albert Gallatin, three of the directors of the "Southern Pacific Branch Railroad Company," who being by me duly sworn, say, that more than one thousand dollars for each and every mile of the railroad proposed and mentioned in the foregoing articles of association, to wit, four hundred and twenty-one thousand ($421,000) dollars have actually and in good faith been subscribed to the capital stock of said company by the persons whose names appear subscribed to the said articles of association, and that ten per cent. on the said amount so subscribed, to wit, forty-two thousand one hundred ($42,100) dollars have actually and in good faith been paid in cash to E. H. Miller, Jr., the treasurer named and appointed by said subscribers from among their number, and that the said subscribers are all known to the said three directors, and to each of them, to be subscribers to said articles of association, and to be the persons so represented.

(Signed)   E. H. MILLER, Jr.
"   ALBERT GALLATIN,
"   C. H. CUMMINGS.

Subscribed and sworn to before me, }
this 23d day of Dec., A. D. 1872, }

(Signed)   CHARLES J. TORBERT,

Notary Public,
in and for Sacramento County,
State of California.

```
...............
:  NOTARIAL  :
:   SEAL.    :
...............
```

IX.

CERTIFIED COPY ARTICLES OF ASSOCIATION, AMALGAMATION AND CONSOLIDATION OF THE SOUTHERN PACIFIC RAILROAD COMPANY AND THE SOUTHERN PACIFIC BRANCH RAILROAD COMPANY·
Endorsed—Filed in the office of the Secretary of State August 19th, 1873.

DRURY MELONE,
Secretary of State.
By H. H. RUSSELL,
Deputy.

STATE OF CALIFORNIA, }
Department of State.

I, Drury Melone, Secretary of State of the State of California, do hereby certify that I have compared the annexed copy of Articles of Association, Amalgamation and Consolidation of the Southern Pacific Railroad Co. with the Southern Pacific Branch Railroad Co., with the original now on file in my office, and that the same is a correct transcript therefrom, and of the whole thereof.

Witness my hand and the great seal of State, at
[SEAL.]   office, in Sacramento, California, the 19th day of August, A. D. 1873.

DRURY MELONE,
Secretary of State.
By H. H. RUSSELL,
Deputy.

ARTICLES OF ASSOCIATION, Amalgamation and Consolidation, made and executed on this the twelfth day of August, A. D. 1873, by and between the Southern Pacific Railroad Company, of the first part, and the Southern Pacific Branch Railroad Company, of the second part.

Witnesseth.—That whereas the said party of the first part, heretofore, to wit, on the eleventh day of October, A. D. 1870, was duly incorporated and organized under the laws of the State of California, by the amalgamation and consolidation of the following railroad corporations, theretofore existing under the laws of said State, to wit, The San Francisco & San Jose Railroad Company, the Santa Clara & Pajaro Valley Railroad Company, The Southern Pacific Railroad Company, and the California Southern Railroad Company, pursuant to articles of amalgamation and consolidation of that date, by them agreed upon, which articles were subsequently amended, to wit, on the eleventh day of April, A. D. 1871, by virtue of the laws of said State, whereby said corporation became duly incorporated and organized under the laws of said State, for the purpose of purchasing, constructing, owning, maintaining and operating a continuous line of railroad from the City of San Francisco, in the State of California, through the City and County of San Francisco, the Counties of San Mateo, Santa Clara, Monterey, Fresno, Tulare, Kern, San Bernardino and San Diego, to some point on the Colorado River, in the south-eastern part of the State of California, a distance of seven hundred and twenty miles, as near as may be. Also, a line of railroad from a point at or near Tehichipa Pass, by way of Los Angeles, to the Texas Pacific Railroad, at or near the Colorado River, a distance of three hundred and twenty-four miles, as near as may be ; also, a line of railroad from the town of Gilroy, in the County of Santa Clara, in said State, passing through said county and the counties of Santa Cruz and Monterey, to a point at or near Salinas City, in said last-named county, a distance of forty-five miles, as near as may be, and also such branches to said lines as the Board of Directors of said corporation may consider advantageous to said corporation, and direct to be established.

And whereas, The said party of the second part was, heretofore, to wit, on the twenty-third day of December, A. D. 1872, duly incorporated and organized under the laws of the State of California, for the purpose of purchasing, constructing, owning, maintaining and operating a railroad from a point on the Southern Pacific Railroad (the railroad of the party of the first part), at or near Salinas City, in the county of Monterey, south-easterly to a point in Kern County, south of Tulare Lake, intersecting the San Joaquin Valley division of the said Southern Pacific Railroad; also, from a point on the above described line, at or near San Miguel, in San Luis Obispo county, thence in a southerly direction to a point of intersection in Los Angeles county with the line of the said Southern Pacific Railroad running from Tehichipa Pass, by way of Los Angeles to Fort Yuma, said roads passing into or through the counties of Monterey, San Luis Obispo, Kern, Santa Barbara and Los Angeles, and said roads, in the aggregate, being as near as may be, four hundred and twenty-eight miles in length.

And whereas, Said parties believe a consolidation and amalgamation of their capital stocks, debts, properties, assets, roads, telegraphs, land and franchises will be mutually advantageous;

And whereas, More than three-fourths in value of all the stockholders in interest of each of said parties have consented, in writing, to such amalgamation and consolidation upon the terms and conditions hereinafter set forth.

Now, therefore, under and by virtue of the statute of the State of California, in such case made and provided, the said parties do hereby mutually covenant and agree, each with the other, to the following articles, to wit:

ARTICLE FIRST.—Said parties do hereby amalgamate and consolidate themselves into a new corporation, under the name and style of the Southern Pacific Railroad Company, which new corporation shall continue in existence for the period of fifty years from the date of these articles; and they do further consolidate and amalgamate their several capital stocks, debts, properties, assets, roads, telegraphs, lands, franchises, rights, titles, privileges, claims and demands of every kind whatsoever, as well in possession as in expectancy, at law or in equity, and do grant, convey and vest the same in the said new corporation, as fully as the same are now severally held and enjoyed by them respectively, subject, however, to all conditions, obligations, stipulations, contracts, agreements, liens, mortgages, incumbrances, judgments, claims and charges thereon or in anywise affecting the same or any part thereof.

ARTICLE SECOND.—The object and purpose of said new corporation shall be to purchase, construct, own, maintain and operate the several lines of railroad hereinbefore described, to wit : a line of railroad from the city of San Francisco, in the State of California, through the city and county of San Francisco, the counties of San Mateo, Santa Clara, Monterey, Fresno, Tulare, Kern, San Bernardino and San Diego to some point on the Colorado River in the southeastern part of the State of California, a distance of seven hundred and twenty miles, as near as may be ; also a line of railroad from a point at or near Tehichipa Pass, by way of Los Angeles to the Texas Pacific Railroad, at or near the Colorado River, passing through the counties of Los Angeles, San Bernardino and San Diego, a distance of three hundred and twenty-four miles, as near as may be ; also a line of railroad from the town of Gilroy, in the county of Santa Clara, in said State, passing through said county and the counties of Santa Cruz and Monterey to a point at or near Salinas City, in said last named county, a distance of forty-five miles, as near as may be ; also a line of railroad from a point on the line thirdly above described at or near Salinas City, in the county of Monterey, southeasterly through said county and into Kern county to a point south of Tulare Lake, in said last named county, intersecting at said point the line of railroad first above described, a distance of one hundred and eighty miles, as near as may be ; also a line of railroad from a point on the last above described line, at or near San Miguel, in the county of San Luis Obispo, thence in a southerly direction through said county, the county of Santa Barbara and into the county of Los Angeles to a point of intersection with the line of railroad secondly above described, to wit : the line from Tehichipa Pass by way of Los Angeles to the Texas Pacific Railroad at or near the Colorado River, a distance of two hundred and forty miles, as near as may be, making in all fifteen hundred and nine miles, as near as may be, and such branches to said lines as the Board of Directors of said new corporation may hereafter from time to time establish.

ARTICLE THIRD.—The Board of Directors of said new corporation shall consist of seven persons, and the following named persons shall act as such directors until their successors shall have been duly elected pursuant to the by-laws of said new corporation hereafter to be adopted, viz. : C. P. Huntington, D. D. Colton, Robert Robinson, Charles Mayne, S. T. Gage, E. H. Miller, Jr., and J. L. Willcutt.

ARTICLE FOURTH.—The capital stock of said new corporation shall be ninety million dollars, divided into nine hundred thousand shares of one hundred dollars each, that sum being the contemplated actual cost of said railroads, including telegraph lines, rolling stock, motive power, shops, depots, etc.

ARTICLE FIFTH.—Each stockholder of each of said parties shall have the same number of shares of the capital stock of the new corporation which he now owns and holds of the capital stock of his respective company, upon the same terms and conditions, and shall be entitled to receive from said new corporation certificates therefor, where the same has been fully paid up, upon the surrender of the certificates now held by him, and where the same has not been fully paid up, he shall receive such other evidence of his ownership as the Board of Directors of said new corporation shall direct, upon the surrender of such evidence of his ownership of such unpaid stock as he may now hold.

ARTICLE SIXTH.—And the said several parties of the first and second parts, each for itself, hereby sells, assigns, transfers, grants, bargains, releases and conveys to the said new and consolidated company and corporation, its successors and assigns forever, all its property, real, personal and mixed of every kind and description, all its capital stock, all its interest in the shares of its capital stock subscribed but not fully paid for; all credits, effects, judgments, decrees, contracts, agreements, claims, dues and demands of every kind and description, and all rights, privileges and franchises, corporate and otherwise, held, owned, or claimed by said parties of the first and second parts, or either of them, in possession or expectancy, either at law or in equity, subject, however, to all conditions, obligations, stipulations, contracts, agreements, liens, mortgages, incumbrances, claims and charges thereon, or in anywise affecting the same.

ARTICLE SEVENTH.—The said new and consolidated company and corporation is to be liable for, and shall fulfill, perform, do and pay all and each of the contracts and agreements, covenants, duties, obligations, liabilities, debts, dues and demands of the said several parties of the first and second parts ; but this amalgamation and consolidation shall not in any way relieve the said parties of the first and second parts, or the stockholders thereof, from any and all just liabilities.

In testimony whereof, the said party of the first part has caused this instrument to be signed by its vice-president (the president being absent) and its secretary, and its corporate seal to be thereunto affixed, and the said party of the second part has caused this instrument to be signed by its president and secretary, and its corporate seal thereunto affixed, in pursuance of orders and resolutions of their several Boards of Directors, made on the twelfth day of August, 1873.

SOUTHERN PACIFIC RAILROAD COMPANY.

(Signed) By DAVID D. COLTON,
Vice-President.

[Corporate Seal.]

(Signed) J. L. WILCUTT,
Secretary.

SOUTHERN PACIFIC BRANCH RAILROAD COMPANY.

By B. R. CROCKER,
President.

[Seal.]

By E. H. MILLER, JR.,
Secretary.

We, the undersigned, being the holders of stock to the extent of more than three-fourths of the value of all stockholders in interest of the said Southern Pacific Railroad Company, party of the first part, to the foregoing new articles of association, amalgamating and consolidating the said parties of the first and second parts, hereby consent to such amalgamation and consolidation and to the said new articles of association, this twelfth day of August, A. D. 1873.

(Signed)   LELAND STANFORD,
CONTRACT AND FINANCE CO.,
Per W. E. BROWN, *Secretary.*
MARK HOPKINS,
ROBERT ROBINSON,
S. T. GAGE,
CHAS. MAYNE,
DAVID D. COLTON,
J. L. WILLCUTT,
E. H. MILLER, JR.

We, the undersigned, being the holders of stock to the extent of more than three-fourths of the value of all stockholders in interest of the said Southern Pacific Branch Railroad Company, party of the second part to the foregoing new articles of association, amalgamating and consolidating the said parties of the first and second parts, hereby consent to such amalgamation and consolidation and to the said new articles of association, this twelfth day of August, A. D. 1873.

(Signed)   LELAND STANFORD,
E. H. MILLER, JR.,
ALBERT GALLATIN,
MARK HOPKINS,
E. W. HOPKINS,
C. H. CUMMINGS,
B. R. CROCKER.

Y.

ARTICLES OF INCORPORATION

OF THE

LOS ANGELES & SAN PEDRO RAILROAD COMPANY.

STATE OF CALIFORNIA, ⎱
    Department of State. ⎰

> U. S. Int. Rev.
> Stamp, 5 cents.

I, H. L. Nichöls, Secretary of State of the State of California, do hereby certify that the annexed is a true, full and correct copy of certificate of incorporation of the Los Angeles & San Pedro Railroad Company, now on file in my office.

> SEAL OF THE
> STATE OF
> CALIFORNIA.

Witness my hand and the great seal of State, at office in Sacramento, California, the ninth day of April, A. D. 1868.

H. L. NICHOLS,
    Secretary of State.
By LEW B. HARRIS,
        Deputy.

We, the undersigned, do hereby form ourselves into an association for the purpose of constructing and maintaining a railroad from the city of Los Angeles, in the county of Los Angeles, State of California, to the bay of San Pedro, its vicinity, and of constructing or purchasing at said bay all necessary wharves and lighters for the use of said road, which said road, as near as can be estimated, will be in length twenty-five miles, and we the undersigned do hereby severally subscribe to the stock of said road, the amounts set opposite to our names, as follows:

John G. Downey, twenty-five hundred dollars in United States gold coin.

John King, twenty-five hundred dollars in United States gold coin.

John S. Griffin, twenty-five hundred dollars in United States gold coin.

J. A. Sanchez, twenty-five hundred dollars in United States gold coin.

P. Beaudry, twenty-five hundred dollars in United States gold coin.

D. W. Alexander, twenty-five hundred dollars in United States gold coin.

Jas. Huber, Jr., twenty-five hundred dollars in United States gold coin.

S. Lazard, twenty-five hundred dollars in United States gold coin.

J. A. Hayward, twenty-five hundred dollars in United States gold coin.

Herman W. Hellman, twenty-five hundred dollars in United States gold coin.

M. Keller, twenty-five hundred dollars in United States gold coin.

Stephen H. Mott, twenty-five hundred dollars in United States gold coin.

O. W. Childs, twenty-five hundred dollars in United States gold coin.

.... dollars in United States gold coin.

.... dollars in United States gold coin.

And we, the undersigned, do hereby appoint Prudent Beaudry as the treasurer of this association.

Given under our hands and seals this 29th day of November, A. D. 1867.

JOHN G. DOWNEY,	[SEAL.]
JOHN S. GRIFFIN,	[SEAL.]
P. BEAUDRY,	[SEAL.]
JOSEPH HUBER, Jr.,	[SEAL.]
F. W. GIBSON,	[SEAL.]
F. P. F. PIMPLE,	[SEAL.]
D. E. HOWARD,	[SEAL.]
HERMAN W. HELLMAN,	[SEAL.]
JOHN KING,	[SEAL.]
J. A. SANCHEZ,	[SEAL.]
D. ALEXANDER,	[SEAL.]
S. LAZARD,	[SEAL.]
J. C. LEUNSEUAIN	[SEAL.]
B. D. WILSON,	[SEAL.]
J. A. HAYWARD,	[SEAL.]
MATHEW KELLER.	[SEAL.]

Receipt of the treasurer of the Los Angeles & San Pedro Railroad Company.

I, Prudent Beaudry, treasurer of said company, as appears from the paper hereto attached, do hereby certify and acknowledge that I have, as treasurer of said company, received from the several stockholders in said company the several amounts set opposite their names as follows :

O. W. Childs, two hundred and fifty dollars in U. S. gold coin.

John King, two hundred and fifty dollars in U. S. gold coin.

John S. Griffin, two hundred and fifty dollars in U. S. gold coin.

P. Beaudry, two hundred and fifty dollars in U. S. gold coin.

D. W. Alexander, two hundred and fifty dollars in U. S. gold coin.

Joseph Huber, Jr., two hundred and fifty dollars in U. S. gold coin.

S. A. Lazard, two hundred and fifty dollars in U. S. gold coin.

Mathew Keller, two hundred and fifty dollars in U. S. gold coin.

H. W. Hellman, two hundred and fifty dollars in U. S. gold coin.

S. H. Mott, two hundred and fifty dollars in U. S. gold coin.

J. G. Downey, two hundred and fifty dollars in U. S. gold coin.

J. A. Hayward, two hundred and fifty dollars in U. S. gold coin.

....in U. S. gold coin.
....in U. S. gold coin.
....in U. S. gold coin.
....in U. S. gold coin.
....in U. S. gold coin.
....in U. S. gold coin.
....in U. S. gold coin.
....in U. S. gold coin.
....in U. S. gold coin.

Given under my hand this 12th day of February, A. D. 1868.

P. BEAUDRY,

{ Int. Rev.
2 cts.
Canceled. }

Treasurer of the Los Angeles & San Pedro Railroad Company.

ARTICLES of ASSOCIATION of the "LOS ANGELES & SAN PEDRO RAILROAD COMPANY."

At a general meeting of the stockholders of the Los Angeles & San Pedro Railroad Company, held at the city of Los Angeles, State of California, on this 12th day of February, A. D. 1868.

Present—The members and stockholders of said company, as follows :

John G. Downey,	John King,	John S. Griffin,
P. Beaudry,	D. W. Alexander,	Joseph Huber, Jr.,
S. Lazard,	J. A. Hayward	H. W. Hellman.
Matthew Keller,	S. H. D. Mott.	

And on the production of the company treasurer's receipt hereto attached for the sum of twenty-five hundred dollars and fifty cents in United States gold coin, the same being in excess of the ten per cent. in cash of the amount required by law to be actually paid on our subscriptions to the capital stock of said railroad company ; we the undersigned hereby waiving the five days' notice of this meeting from the said company treasurer, as provided by law, do hereby make and adopt the following articles of association :

ARTICLE I. The corporate name of this association is, and shall be, "The Los Angeles & San Pedro Railroad Company."

ARTICLE II. The amount of the capital stock of this corporation is, and shall be, the sum of five hundred thousand ($500,000) dollars in United States gold coin, and the same shall be divided into shares of one hundred dollars each, of like gold coin of the United States; which said sum of five hundred thousand dollars in United States gold coin is the actual contemplated cost of constructing said railroad from the city of Los Angeles, in the county of Los Angeles, State of California, to the Bay of San Pedro, in said county, together with the cost of right of way, motive power and construction or purchase of wharf and lighters at the bay of San Pedro, and for every other appurtenance and thing, as nearly as can be estimated by competent engineers.

ARTICLE III. The number of directors who are to manage the affairs of said railroad company, until others are elected at the first company meeting hereafter held, as shall be provided by the "By-Laws" of this company, shall be five, and their names are as follows:

John G. Downey,	D. W. Alexander,	J. S. Griffin.
John King,	Matthew Keller,	

ARTICLE IV. The Los Angeles & San Pedro Railroad Company is to extend from the city of Los Angeles, in the county of Los Angeles, State of California, to a point on or near the bay of San Pedro, in said county, and the length of said road is to be, as near as may be, the distance of twenty-five miles.

ARTICLE V. The principal place of business of said corporation is intended to be, and shall be, at the city of Los Angeles, in the county of Los Angeles, State of California.

ARTICLE VI. This corporation shall continue for the period of 49 years from the 12th day of February, A. D. 1868.

We, the subscribers, in testimony of the above and in pursuance of law, do hereunto personally and severally subscribe our names, with our several places of residence and the several shares of stock taken by us in said company set opposite to our names.

D. W. Alexander, of Los Angeles, twenty-five (25) shares.
John S. Griffin, of Los Angeles, twenty-five (25) shares.
Joseph Huber, Jr., of Los Angeles, twenty-five (25) shares.
John G. Downey, of   twenty-five (25) shares.
John King, of Los Angeles, twenty-five (25) shares.
O. W. Childs, of Los Angeles, twenty-five (25) shares.
Herman W. Hellman, of Los Angeles, twenty-five (25) shares.
P. Beaudry, of Los Angeles, twenty-five (25) shares.
S. Lazard, of Los Angeles, twenty-five (25) shares.
Jas. A. Hayward, of Los Angeles, twenty-five (25) shares.
Matthew Keller, of Los Angeles, twenty-five (25) shares.

Stephen H. Mott, of Los Angeles, twenty-five (25) shares.

of	shares.
of	shares.
of	shares.
of	shares.
of	shares.
of	shares.
of	shares.

STATE OF CALIFORNIA, ⎱ ss.:
County of Los Angeles, ⎰

This day, John G. Downey, Matthew Keller and John King, parties whose names are signed to the foregoing articles of association and to me well known, personally appeared before the undersigned at the said county, and being duly sworn on oath, say, each for himself and not for the other, that the said sum of twenty-five hundred and $\frac{50}{100}$ dollars in U. S. gold coin, of the stock of the Los Angeles & San Pedro Railroad Company has been subscribed, and that ten per cent. in cash thereon, in like gold coin, has actually and in good faith been paid over to the treasurer of said company, and that the subscribers to said articles are all known by said affiants to be subscribers thereto, and to be the persons so represented, and that said affiants are directors in said company.

{ Int. Rev. Stamp,
  5 cents,
  canceled. }

Given under my hand, this 12th day of February, A. D. 1868.

MATTHEW KELLER,
JOHN KING,
JOHN G. DOWNEY.

Sworn and subscribed to before me, ⎱
 this 12th day of February, 1868, ⎰
 [SEAL.]   GEO. J. CLARK,
       Notary Public.

(Endorsed.)—Los Angeles & San Pedro Railroad Company, Articles of Incorporation.—Filed in the office of the secretary of State, February 18th, 1868, H. L. Nichols, Sec. of State, by Lew B. Harris, Dep.

{ 5 cent
  Int. Rev. Stamp,
  canceled. }

XI.

CERTIFIED COPY ARTICLES OF ASSOCIATION, AMALGAMATION AND CONSOLIDATION OF THE SOUTHERN PACIFIC RAILROAD COMPANY AND THE LOS ANGELES & SAN PEDRO RAILROAD COMPANY.

Endorsed—Filed in the office of the Secretary of State, Dec. 18th, 1874.

DRURY MELONE,
Secretary of State.

By N. E. WHITE.

STATE OF CALIFORNIA, }
Department of State. }

I, Drury Melone, Secretary of State of the State of California, do hereby certify that I have compared the annexed copy of Articles of Association, Amalgamation and Consolidation, with the original now on file in my office, and that the same is a correct transcript therefrom, and of the whole thereof.

Witness my hand and the great seal of State, at office, in Sacramento, California, the 18th day of December, A. D. 1874.

[SEAL.]

DRURY MELONE,
Secretary of State.

By N. E. WHITE,
Deputy.

ARTICLES OF ASSOCIATION, Amalgamation and Consolidation, made and executed this 17th day of December, A. D. 1874, by and between the Southern Pacific Railroad Company, of the first part, and the Los Angeles and San Pedro Railroad Company, party of the second part : Witnesseth, that whereas, the said party of the first part, heretofore, to wit—on the 19th day of August, A D. 1873, was duly incorporated and organized under the law of the State of California, by the amalgamation and consolidation of the following railroad corporations, theretofore existing under laws of said state, to wit : The San Francisco & San Jose Railroad Company, the Santa Clara

& Pajaro Railroad Company, the Southern Pacific Railroad Company, the California Southern Railroad Company, and the Southern Pacific Branch Railroad Company, all of said railroad companies being incorporated and duly organized under the laws of the State of California, prior to the 31st day of December, A. D. 1872, pursuant to articles of amalgamation and consolidation of that date by them agreed upon, which, by virtue of the law of said State, entitled " an Act to provide for the Incorporation of Railroad Companies and the Management of the affairs thereof, and other matters relating thereto," approved May 20th, 1861, whereby said corporation became duly incorporated and organized under the laws of said state for the purposes of purchasing, constructing, owning, maintaining and operating continuous lines of railroad from the city and county of San Francisco, in the State of California, through the city and county of San Francisco, the counties of San Mateo, Santa Clara, Monterey, Fresno, Tulare, Kern, San Bernardino and San Diego, to some point on the Colorado River, in the southeastern part of the State of California, a distance of six hundred and thirty-five and $\frac{87}{100}$ miles, as near as may be ; also a line of railroad from a point at or near Tehachapa Pass, by way of Los Angeles, to the Texas Pacific Railroad, at or near the Colorado River, a distance of three hundred and fifty-six and $\frac{7}{100}$ miles, as near as may be; also a line of railroad from the town of Gilroy, in the county of Santa Clara, in said state, passing through said county, and the counties of Santa Cruz and Monterey, to a point at or near Salinas City, in said last named county, a distance of thirty-five and $\frac{1}{10}$ miles, as near as may be, and also such branches to said lines as the Board of Directors of said corporation may consider advantageous to said corporation and direct to be established ; and also from a point on said road aforesaid, at or near Salinas City, in the county of Monterey, southerly to a point in Kern county, south of Tulare Lake, intersecting the San Joaquin division of the said Southern Pacific Railroad; also from a point on the above described line, at or near San Miguel, in San Luis Obispo county ; thence in a southerly direction to a point of intersection in Los Angeles county, with the line of the said Southern Pacific Railroad, running from Tehachapa Pass, by way of Los Angeles to Fort Yuma; said roads passing into or through the counties of Monterey, San Luis Obispo, Kern, Santa Barbara, and Los Angeles; and said roads, in the aggregate, being as near as may be, four hundred and two (402) miles in length.

And whereas, the said party of the second part was heretofore, to wit, on the 18th day of February, A. D. 1868, duly incorporated and organized under the laws of the State of California, for the purpose of constructing, owning and maintaining and operating a railroad from a point in the city of Los Angeles, in the county of Los Angeles, State of California, to a point on or near the Bay of San Pedro, in said county, a distance of twenty and $\frac{6}{10}$ miles.

And whereas, said parties believe a consolidation and amalgamation of their capital stock, debts, properties, assets, roads, telegraphs, lands and franchises will be mutually advantageous;

And whereas, more than three-fourths in value of the stockholders in interest of each of said parties, have consented in writing to such amalgamation and consolidation upon the terms and conditions hereinafter set forth;

And whereas, all of the railroad corporations included in the several consolidations were duly incorporated prior to the 31st day of December, A. D. 1872.

Now, therefore, under and by virtue of the fortieth section of a law of the State of California, entitled "An Act to provide for the incorporation of railroad companies, and the management of the affairs thereof, and other matters relating thereto," approved May 20th, 1861, and the several amendments thereto, the said parties do hereby mutually covenant and agree, each with the other, to the following articles, to wit:

ARTICLE FIRST.—Said parties do hereby amalgamate and consolidate themselves into a new corporation under the name and style of the Southern Pacific Railroad Company, which new corporation shall continue in existence for the period of fifty years from the date of these articles; and they do further consolidate and amalgamate their several capital stocks, debts, properties, assets, roads, telegraphs, lands, franchises, rights, titles, privileges, claims and demands of every kind whatsoever, as well in possession as in expectancy, at law or in equity, and do grant, convey and vest the same in the said new corporation, as fully as the same are now severally held and enjoyed by them respectively, subject, however, to all conditions, obligations, stipulations, contracts, agreements, liens, mortgages, incumbrances, judgments, claims and charges thereon or in anywise affecting the same or any part thereof.

ARTICLE SECOND.—The object and purpose of said new corporation shall be to purchase, construct, own, maintain and operate the several lines of railroad hereinbefore described, to wit: Continuous lines of railroad from the city and county of San Francisco, in the State of California, through the city and county of San Francisco, the counties of San Mateo, Santa Clara, Monterey, Fresno, Tulare, Kern, San Bernardino and San Diego, to some point on the Colorado River, in the southeastern part of the State of California, a distance of six hundred and thirty-five and $\frac{8.7}{100}$ miles, as near as may be; also a line of railroad from a point at or near Tehachapa Pass by way of Los Angeles, to the Texas Pacific Railroad, at or near the Colorado River, a distance of three hundred and fifty-six and $\frac{7}{10}$ miles, as near as may be; also a line of railroad from the town of Gilroy, in the county of Santa Clara, in said State, passing through said county, and the counties of Santa Cruz and Monterey, to a point at or near Salinas City, in said last named county, a distance of thirty-five and $\frac{1}{10}$ miles, as near as may be, and also such branches to said lines as the Board of Directors of said corporation may consider advantageous to said corporation, and direct to be established. And also from a point on said road aforesaid, at or near Salinas city, in the county of Monterey, southerly to a point in Kern county, south of Tulare Lake, intersecting the San Joaquin Division of the said Southern Pacific Railroad; also from a point on the above described line, at or near San Miguel, in San Luis

Obispo county ; thence in a southerly direction to a point of intersection in Los Angeles county, with the line of the said Southern Pacific Railroad, running from Tehachapa Pass by way of Los Angeles to Fort Yuma ; said roads passing into or through the counties of Monterey, San Luis Obispo, Kern, Santa Barbara and Los Angeles, and said roads, in the aggregate, being as near as may be, four hundred and two miles in length ; also from a point in the city of Los Angeles, in the county of Los Angeles, State of California, to a point on or near the Bay of San Pedro, in said county, a distance of twenty and one-half miles. The aggregate length of all of said railroads being one thousand four hundred and forty-nine and fifty-four one hundredths miles.

ARTICLE THIRD.—The Board of Directors of said new corporation shall consist of seven persons, and the following named persons shall act as such Directors until their successors shall have been duly elected pursuant to the by-laws of said new corporation hereafter to be adopted, viz.: Charles Crocker, David D. Colton, E. H. Miller, Jr., Robert Robinson, Nicholas T. Smith, Stephen T. Gage and Joseph L. Willcutt.

ARTICLE FOURTH.—The capital stock of said new corporation shall be ninety millions of dollars, divided into nine hundred thousand shares of one hundred dollars each, that sum being the contemplated actual cost of said railroads, including telegraph lines, rolling stock, motive power, shops, depots, &c.

ARTICLE FIFTH.—Each stockholder of each of said parties shall have the same number of shares of the capital stock of the new corporation which he now owns and holds of the capital stock of his respective company, upon the same terms and conditions, and shall be entitled to receive from said new corporation certificates therefor, where the same has been fully paid up, upon the surrender of the certificates now held by him, and where the same has not been fully paid up, he shall receive such other evidence of his ownership as the Board of Directors of said new corporation shall direct, upon the surrender of such evidence of his ownership of such unpaid stock as he may now hold.

ARTICLE SIXTH.—And the said several parties of the first and second parts, each for itself, hereby sells, assigns, transfers, grants, bargains, releases and conveys to the said new and consolidated company and corporation, its successors and assigns forever, all its property, real, personal and mixed, of every kind and description ; all its capital stock, all its interest in the shares of its capital stock subscribed, but not fully paid up ; all credits, effects, judgments, decrees, contracts, agreements, claims, dues and demands of every kind and description, and all rights, privileges and franchises, corporate and otherwise, held, owned or claimed by said parties of the first and second parts or either of them, in possession or expectancy, either at law or in equity, subject, however, to all conditions, obligations, stipulations, contracts, agreements, liens, mortgages, incumbrances, claims and charges thereon, or in anywise affecting the same.

ARTICLE SEVENTH.—The said new and consolidated company and corporation is to be liable for, and shall fulfill, perform, do and pay all and each of the contracts and agreements, covenants, duties, obligations, liabilities, debts, dues and demands of the said several parties of the first and second parts, but this amalgamation and consolidation shall not, in any way, relieve the said parties of the first and second parts, or the stockholders thereof, from any and all just liabilities.

In testimony whereof, the said party of the first part has caused this instrument to be signed by its President and Secretary, and its corporate seal to be hereunto affixed ; and the said party of the second part has caused this instrument to be signed by its President and Secretary, and its Corporate Seal hereunto affixed, in pursuance of orders and resolutions of their several Boards of

Directors, made on the seventeenth day of December, A. D. 1874.

```
. . . . . . . . . . . .
:    Seal         :
: Southern Pacific :
:    R. R. Co.    :
. . . . . . . . . . . .
```

SOUTHERN PACIFIC RAILROAD
COMPANY,
By CHARLES CROCKER,
President.

J. L. WILLCUTT,
Secretary.

```
.  . . . . . . . . . .
:    Seal         :
:  Los Angeles    :
:      and        :
:   San Pedro     :
:    R. R. Co.    :
. . . . . . . . . . .
```

LOS ANGELES AND SAN PEDRO
RAILROAD COMPANY,
By LELAND STANFORD,
President.

J. L. WILLCUTT,
Secretary.

We, the undersigned, being the holders of stock to the extent of more than three-fourths of the value of all stockholders in interest of the said Southern Pacific Railroad Company, party of the first part to the aforegoing new articles of association, amalgamating and consolidating the said parties of the first and second parts, hereby consent to such amalgamation and consolidation, and to the said new articles of association, this seventeenth day of December, A. D. 1874.

CHARLES CROCKER,
S. T. GAGE,
N. T. SMITH,
DAVID D. COLTON,
E. H. MILLER, Jr.,
J. L. WILLCUTT,
ROBERT ROBINSON,
MARK HOPKINS,
LELAND STANFORD,
C. P. HUNTINGTON,
By MARK HOPKINS,
Attorney in Fact.
CONTRACT AND FINANCE CO.,
By JNO. MILLER,
Secretary.

We, the undersigned, being the holders of stock to the extent of more than three-fourths of the value of all stockholders in interest of the said Los Angeles & San Pedro Railroad Company, party of the second part, to the foregoing new articles of association, amalgamating and consolidating the said parties of the first and second parts, hereby consent to such amalgamation and consolidation, and to the said new articles of association, this seventeenth day of December, A. D. 1874.

LELAND STANFORD,
CHARLES CROCKER,
DAVID D. COLTON,
MARK HOPKINS,
C. P. HUNTINGTON,
By MARK HOPKINS,
Attorney in Fact.
ROBERT ROBINSON,
J. L. WILLCUTT,
CONTRACT AND FINANCE CO.,
By JNO. MILLER,
Secretary.